One Day

Vivienne Gerard

One Day

My Soul Journey in the Gaia Tribe

Vivienne Gerard

For My Soul Family

The Ones holding Space for me throughout Time, and the Physical Ones walking this lifetime's Soul Journey by my side.

So Much Love....

ONE DAY. Copyright © 2017 by Vivienne Gerard.

All rights reserved. Printed in the United States of America. First Printing April 2017. No part of this book may be used or reproduced in any manner whatsoever without written permission except in the case of brief quotations embodied in critical articles and reviews. None of the content in this book is provided as medical or other health care advice. Please contact your health care provider directly for the appropriate information and any related advice.

For information, visit **www.mysouljourney.com**.

ISBN: 069287738X
ISBN: 978-0692877388

ONE DAY
My Soul Journey in the Gaia Tribe

	Prologue	9
1	The Beginning	11
2	Integration	15
3	Introduction to Dimensions	23
4	Fourth Dimension	45
5	Fifth Dimension	67
6	Sixth Dimension	85
7	Seventh Dimension	109
8	Eighth Dimension	131
9	Ninth Dimension	151
10	Tenth Dimension	169
11-12	Eleventh & Twelfth Dimensions	183
13-14	Thirteenth & Fourteenth Dimensions	197
15+	Fifteenth Dimension & Beyond	213
	Epilogue	217
	Resources	219
	The Soul Filters' Story	225

PROLOGUE

SOUND HEALING INTEGRATION:

Snatam Kaur
(and Guru Ganesha Singh)

Ong Namo

We begin our journey together with Sound... just as My Soul Journey started in the very beginning. xoxo

Vivienne Gerard

1

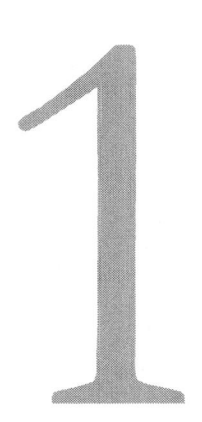

THE BEGINNING

"Ong"

Vivienne Gerard

THE BEGINNING

In the beginning, there was nothing.

Nothing existed.

Until a spark, a spark of creativity, of magic happened.

And Light came into the Void, the Darkness.

The Light came with Sound, and the Sound was **Ong**.

Ong.

Ong.

It meant **I Am**.

I Am.

I Exist.

I Am Here.

I Am Breath.

I Am Sound.

I AM.

And with that first spark, that first breath, that first creative energy, more could form.

MORE.

More could form.

And it did through expansion.

More formed through expansion.

Expansion of Sound.

Expansion of Breath.

And Expansion of Light.

And so in the darkness, One Light became more Light.

That first expansion went from One to Seven. The Original and then the Six Elders, who came to stand beside the first Original Breath.

Seven became the magical number. One plus Six created Seven and all were equal. All came from the Original… so how could they be anything but equal?

They were One… how could they be anything separate?

And the Seven were Sound and Light. And they expanded. They expanded Sound and Light. They added on the other Sounds.

Namo.

It meant **I Bow.**

Ong Namo.

I Bow to the Divine Teacher Within.

Each… Each of the Six had a unique Sound and from that unique Sound, the Tribe would form. And when the Tribe heard that Sound, they would know they were Home.

So I can only speak of my Tribe and our Sound is Ong Namo.

Ong *- for the Original, very first Breath.*

Namo *– for the Brave One who came after the Ong and started her own Tribe.*

The others will need to speak for themselves, I speak only for mine.

2

INTEGRATION

"All"

Vivienne Gerard

INTEGRATION

The delight, the joy, the pleasure of a Soul is to continue expanding into more. To always be Becoming More. Allowing creativity to flow through to create new… to create things that have never existed before.

That is the delight of Soul work.

When we choose as Souls to have human incarnations, it is because the dance of physical and spiritual-energetic together creates in ways that expand outside of just the spiritual. Every human incarnation we have as a Soul allows us to be new, be more, and be expanded.

We have been playing this dance of humanity, of physical and spiritual combining for many, many years and lifetimes.

Now we arrive here at the edge of the physical limitations of our planet Earth and it is time for us to expand our consciousness. To wake up to our consciousness so that we can allow for a shift to happen on our planet.

To heal. To realign the energy and the heartbeat.

The pace of our planet is too fast, too intense.

The expansion is too rapid for what our physical planet can maintain. And so there is a change that we are undergoing, starting in this year of 2017 and onward.

And we are co-creating it together.

There is no one person who is going to have an answer or a solution that fixes everything. There are just many

Souls, many guides here on this planet and around our planet energetically who are co-creating what happens next.

Whether we are aware of it or not, choose it or not, like it or not, or actively participate or not, consciousness is expanding and is going to continue expanding.

Humanity is going to reach a point where the physical cannot continue functioning on this planet in the way that we have been used to, and the spiritual and the physical are going to re-align in a way that we are all co-creating, whether we are aware of it or not.

One of my Soul gifts that I bring to our planet during this time of change is a steady alignment and connection to the heartbeat of our Earth to help it align with the heartbeat of the Universe as we slow down.

Another of my Soul gifts is to match the rhythms and tune into the ways that we can partner with our planet… co-create with our planet… to slow down the pace of humanity.

Everyone is going to have their own gifts that they bring and their own way of sharing those gifts. My focus is simply on what I know and what I can bring and share: understanding consciousness and understanding how these dimensional shifts I am going to describe can tune us into Universal Energy, Universal Love, and Harmony.

That gift when it's shared can help millions, billions of people. Not because I have the answer or I do all the work, but because I share this information and then allow everyone who receives it to co-create along with me THEIR solution, take THEIR inspired action, and share THEIR gifts.

I cannot shift all of humanity through the levels of consciousness, but I can talk about it and create a bridge so that each individual if they choose, can find their own way into that expanded pathway of consciousness.

So why care?

Why get engaged? Why take action?

That is the individual choice of each Soul-human. You can read this book, hear this information, or watch a recommended video link and not resonate with any of it and just put it aside. That's every individual's choice.

But this planet is going to hit the physical limitations of time and space and the density of matter whether you agree or align with it or not.

And so the empowered place to be is to EXPLORE whatever comes up as you receive this information.

Do your own investigation, your own tuning into the quiet voice inside of you.

Listen and explore it all.

Sit and contemplate whatever ideas come up inside of you as you hear other people's ideas.

Then when you have clarity, take inspired action on your OWN clarity.

Sitting and watching from the sidelines keeps you passively waiting, assuming all is going to just continue to unfold in time and turn out okay.

VIDEO HEALING INTEGRATION:
National Geographic Channel
"Before the Flood"

If nothing else, our Earth is proving to us that we can't continue to do that. Our weather patterns are already disrupted. Our water supplies are already getting contaminated. The temperature is already rising.

Our planet is going to shake us awake, whether we like it or not.

It is always a choice for each individual if you want to open your eyes, ears, heart and Soul, and step into this lifedance of physical and spiritual more actively. But time is going to move us along regardless of your engagement.

So my hope is that the information in this book inspires you first, and most importantly, to Be Still. To tune into your own knowing. To explore other resources. To follow the trail wherever this inquiry takes you.

And then share what you find.

Make a YouTube video, write a blog post, write a book, make a movie, or create art.

Share.

Share what comes to you.

Let us all learn from each other, all co-create together.

From what I understand and can see of our individual evolutions through these dimensions of consciousness - the faster that this collaborative process happens then the more direct our humanity's access is to Universal knowledge, to Universal truths, to solutions beyond what our limited and physical minds can see in this moment.

If LOTS of people are all evolving rapidly together and if we are all getting quiet and tapping into that collective consciousness wealth of information, then we can all start bringing our nuggets, our pieces of wisdom together and the solutions will seamlessly flow.

Groups will naturally gather to create and mold solutions. Communities of individuals who are all tapped in and listening will form, tuning into their knowledge and then creating something that has not been addressed in that way before.

And climate change suddenly becomes something we can solve.

Poverty becomes something that is eradicated.

Hunger...

Hunger goes away.

Because we are all co-creating from a place of empowerment, from a place of tapping into Universal knowledge and collective consciousness.

> **The Pathway to Healing Our Planet Feels like this Exploration of Dimensions of Consciousness First at an *Individual* Level.**

As you move through the dimensions of consciousness, compare with what I have written and add your notes, create new notes, write new chapters for yourself...

Share how your experience of it is different than my experience of it. Your experience might resonate with a million other people who have a similar experience that perhaps doesn't quite match what I experienced!

All of these voices being shared with respect, with truth, and with clarity can resonate on larger and wider scales.

And we have a global healing movement.

A momentum for collaborative co-creation and change.

And our planet becomes Paradise.

SOUND HEALING INTEGRATION:
The Ho'oponopono Song

Becomes this beautiful blend of spiritual and physical of which we have only dreamed.

And it happens rapidly.

Within this generation…

It is with so much love in my heart that I offer you this pathway into Your Own Journey.

ONE DAY

INTRODUCTION TO CONSCIOUSNESS AND DIMENSIONS

3rd - "Density, Fear"

Vivienne Gerard

INTRODUCTION TO CONSCIOUSNESS AND DIMENSIONS

Consciousness is the spark of Creativity. Breath. Existence. And it is always expanding, has always been expanding.

It is a curious thing to try explain, as it is constantly changing. One person's definition of it in one moment is instantly different in the next moment. And completely different for another person in either of those moments!

I have wondered how to share my definition, knowing that it will not match anyone else's experience of it fully. Now is the time, though, for these deeper moments of sharing our stories and beliefs in order to help us find how we are perhaps the same. Find those places where we can agree, share our Truth, and begin building the foundations for the solutions that our planet needs from us.

What feels important then, as we begin this journey into new understandings together, is a suggestion of how to become clear about our own unique definitions and Truth.

My answer is simple.

Truth resonates.

It has a vibration that is strong and powerful.

When Truth is shared, energy is physically and emotionally released. We have all at times felt Truth reach through our emotional walls and rigid belief systems... it is a tangible shiver of the spine or immediate tears flowing down your face. Truth can be felt as a punch in the solar plexus chakra – the "gut" of your physical body. It is experienced as an opening of the heart, a warming sensation spreading through your chest.

There is a knowing in your Soul when you hear someone speaking their Truth, even if it is information you have not heard before.

I invite you to open your heart and hear my Truth.

To introduce consciousness as I understand it, I must go back... far back in my Soul story.

Back to The Beginning.

All the way back to Ong Namo.

The Elder who wanted to play with time and space and the density of matter – among many other things of which I do not know. I only know that which I came into... Ong Namo who breathed my Tribe into existence as She thought and created us.

As consciousness, Her consciousness, expanded and we were formed.

From One plus Six which created Seven – we then expanded and went to 21. We were the third layer of consciousness expanding.

My first breath, my first awareness was sound. The vibration that I could feel.

Ong.

The Universe is made up of sound. Every level of consciousness, every aspect of consciousness has a sound. And the void at the very beginning was no sound until the Original Source created the first sound of Ong – "I Am."

As consciousness expanded... sound expanded... the Universe expanded.

I remember sound. I remember vibration.

I remember feeling connection from the very beginning. There were fourteen of us, together.

We were all breathed into existence with the same intention, the same consciousness: **Gaia Tribe to play with Time, Space, and the Density of Matter.**

Our Elders taught us. They took on form and they played with us. They showed us Stars and Planets and Rings and Moons and Constellations and Nebulas. They just played!

As they delighted in our enjoyment of the play, new sparks of creativity were formed. And the Universe expanded and took on form and became lighter. The Void became filled with Light in all these different forms and sounds. The sounds continued to guide us. And we played! We played and we played!

Time wasn't something. It didn't exist.

Time does not exist.

Our assignment was to play with Time, which is why we are called the Time Keepers. And Time is experienced through Space and the Density of Matter. Because Matter is Finite.

As we expanded consciousness and delighted in the magic of the mystery that we were all co-creating as the Gaia Time Keepers, we started to play with Matter through elements. We brought together Hydrogen and Helium and we delighted in watching them explode!

Then we found that Matter came from that explosion and we could bring it back together and form it and it would stick. As with all play, it was all for the delight — the delight of the magic of it.

The beauty of New.

The beauty of Creation.

Every expansion is for the beauty of creation of New... of more existing than existed before.

And so **Ong Namo's Gaia Time Keeper Tribe** *created*

form. Created this planet that we call Earth. It was our Joy. Our Delight. Our Gift to expanding consciousness. To create form, to create Magic from the density of Matter.

We set up a classroom. We set up a sacred roundtable where the fourteen of us would gather, still gather, do gather, are gathering. I know all fourteen, holding sacred space for this planet that we Are and that we Love.

And in the center is Source.

Ong – the Original Breath is the Center of consciousness of Earth. And the six Elders stand around the Earth. Of course. Source and the Elders are on every planet, every star. They are One with all of us, Always. We are One.

This planet came from our consciousness.

It came from Source, and so it IS One Breath. As our planet breathes, all who came from Ong Namo breathe.

We are one original sound, one original breath.

Sound.

Sound and breath unite us.

> SOUND HEALING INTEGRATION:
> Ashana
> "Into Your Arms"

And so we formed Earth, the 21 Time Keepers. We formed Earth carefully. "Carefully – with great care." With Precision. With Consciousness. We formed this planet.

We started, like all creations that are formed like a star, with Helium and Hydrogen and a little mixture of magic. Which is Belief. Trust. Thought. The Earth in its original form looked like our moon. It was a rocky, uninhabitable collection of stardust. We kept that original thought form and held it as our moon as a reminder, as a balancer for Earth.

The moon would hold the original darkness, the original light. It would bring light and shadow together. It would set the rhythm of the Earth that came in our second thought. The first original thought is our moon, which is why humans have always tried to reach the moon. They are reaching back through time and space to the original thought of their planet.

We gathered and analyzed and thought and dreamed and played... and we breathed into existence... Gaia. What we know now as Gaia.

Gaia. Earth.

It was a Star. In form. With a bubble around it to protect it from other thought forms. It was an energy bubble. We created an energy field around our planet to hold in all that would be created within that bubble. We created a cocoon, a womb.

Gaia was birthed from the womb of the Time Keepers. And the womb stayed.

Our intention was that Gaia would be a space for creativity to expand and multiply within the energy field that we created. That creativity would multiply and expand in this incubator. So we breathed that energy field into the consciousness of Earth.

> SOUND HEALING INTEGRATION:
> Deuter
> "Gaia Dreaming Herself Awake"

And all that would happen within this bubble, it came from Ong Namo. It resonated with Ong Namo.

There are others who work with their Elders and others who work with our Elder. And yet that is not my story to share.

I will speak of what I know, which is this planet I love called Gaia. And the expansion of consciousness here in the physical.

Consciousness evolves in phases, levels, dimensions. As our human brains attempt to put some structure and form to a concept that is formless, numbers become useful. They provide a way to measure and evaluate progress or movement along a continuum.

The rest of this book is about my understanding and experience of how consciousness evolves through dimensional levels, using numbers to help give structure and provide guidance along your path.

For our journey together here, my attention is primarily focusing on the expansion of consciousness for humans *(third and above)*.

So, here we go...

Dimensions feel like energy levels:

The First dimension includes plants, elements, chemistry, matter, earth, dirt, clouds, sky, trees, rocks... the basic level of biology or bio-life. The foundational level of energizing force where Earth's recycling happens. There is so much untapped wisdom in this first dimension of consciousness that humanity is only beginning to understand.

The Second dimension includes animals - fish, mammals, dogs, cats, horses, alligators, whales... any form of non-human life that procreates, has rebirth, continues, or has a digestive system. The animal brings in energy, processes it, uses it, creates waste, and then births new life. So a pro-creational source of energy.

One of the best Guides I know for this dimension of consciousness is my Soul Friend, Jo. I asked for her wisdom about the beings of the second dimension and have her permission to share these beautiful reflections.

"Now. The real gift of the second dimension is their ability to live in the Now.

Their love, affection, fear, etc. is in the purity of the moment with no projection, concern or manipulation of future outcomes. To me, one of the bonuses of that is to help ground those in the third (humans!) who can lose their way.

Animals, for me, are an anchor of purity and grounding from my day-to-day outer purpose. My mind can function in overdrive and that helps me "succeed" in a society like ours. Without their simplicity and truth, I would be a corporate zombie. They are teachers. They are touchstones.

I also believe there are several dimensions to animals *(2.A, 2.B, 2.C?)* and that the more evolved ones remain with our Soul groups, along with human Soul family. The animals I'm referring to have a combination of a larger cerebral cortex and exposure to their human counterparts or exposure to a wild yet safe environment. Typically with family or pack dynamics (elephants), they have a larger capacity for emotion than perhaps a fish *(although I'm open to being wrong there)*. A healthy co-existence with humans lets them evolve the more heart-centered side of themselves, as they will be less encumbered by the lower issues on Maslow's hierarchy of needs like basic survival. While I don't believe they have the capacity to evolve to the top, I know with certainty that love and connection are possible.

And that is where a beautiful exchange can happen.

We provide security and they return love – but in a unique way from human love. Their behavior mirrors and teaches us what many of the great Masters have told us for generations.

They don't feel responsibility for filling us up out of guilt, obligation or because of social pressures.

They love us when they want, when it's authentic

and they leave it to us to do the inner work of loving ourselves first and foremost.

My belief is that the purity and simplicity of the relationships combined with their relative shorter life spans make it possible for us to have the same animal Soul appear to us multiple times in one human lifetime. I believe that has happened to me.

Are they all fun and games? No. Animals exposed to terror or deprivation of some kind suffer lack of development, just as humans do. Or maybe they're wired with a personality or temperament that stunts their opportunity for whatever reason. This is one of the reasons it puzzles me when people don't like dogs or cats as a general species. There are loving, hysterical, and adoring personalities in every species. And some are just jerks. Some are more work than others, so the closer they are to human constraints, (a house with items not to chew on, shed in, visitors to jump on, etc.) the more distracted the connection can sometimes be.

Because they are so tied to the Now and live so authentically, in one sense these beings are purer and therefore closer to Source at any given time. How beautiful. Less evolved, but closer to Source more of the time. Third allows for awareness and expanded consciousness, but it can get REALLY muddied with thought and ego."

The Third dimension is the first level of human consciousness. So there's a thinking brain that can create ideas. Hands that can mold and shape new ideas. There's a complex digestive system that thinks for itself, brings in ideas and nutrients and processes waste.

The third dimension feels like the reality of the physical experience for most people here on Earth. For lifetimes (thousands of years), the third dimension has been the reality that the majority of incarnated Souls in human bodies have experienced.

When a Soul decides to incarnate (take on human form), they arrive into a third-dimensional reality that is dense, heavy, and limited in what you can see and understand. The […] are functioning but perhaps blocked or not […] energy at the optimal level of what a body and a […] create.

[…] long time on Earth, life wasn't as dense as it feels […] ith more and more Souls incarnating on this planet, […] their energy and auras into the physical, the […] of the planet has become heavier and the […] on of energy has become tighter. The third […] on is feeling more limited, more restrictive than […] ore.

[…] e third dimension, a Soul-human feels the […] e society's energy as their baseline, their "norm." It […] that life can be scary, or your experiences are […] be limited, or there's going to be lack. You tend to […] with the average person in the average crowd […] e average life. You don't set your expectations too […] use then you're going to be disappointed. […] ing lots of warnings that many of us grew up with […] eration and those before us (it's finally shifting […] ew generations, thankfully!).

[…] ample, we might have been hearing *"Don't get too […] e going to fall,"* *"Don't let your ego expand too much or you're going to be disappointed,"* *"Don't set the bar too high because it's going to come crashing down on you,"* or *"There's never going to be enough for everyone."*

These phrases and limitations are so common that we stop questioning why life feels difficult and we have to work really hard. The news media supports this mentality by constantly showing us the "bad" stories. Our communities keep these messages right in front of us so that we don't forget. And so we stay in this limited experience of the third dimension.

I believe we choose that limited experience of life.

I believe that our Souls know coming into each human incarnation that there is this feeling of density with a limited thought process. And that it exists to push against us, to ignite the spark of commitment and creativity and desire to push PAST that limitation into the possibilities of what others aren't expecting or thinking is possible yet.

I believe we choose this dense third dimension of consciousness. We choose that we're going to come into a human body and have this experience of being told no all the time. Because in being told no, we can also find the strength to push back with our own *"NO!"* And this time, we add *"Oh, and also... I'm going to show you that I can create my OWN Yes!"*

But until then, in the third-dimensional reality, we're like sheep that keep moving in a flock together, following the rules, following the systems and the structures. Making sure that we don't ruffle too many feathers.

We stay safe by staying small. By limiting our options. And it feels good because everyone else is just like us.

MY "FLOCK" STORY

When I was younger, we moved around a lot, often changing schools. I was usually the new girl coming into the collective group that was already in each school. A group with their own established norms and patterns, hierarchy, and routines.

I would come in as the new student and typically be excluded from the group for a while because they were figuring me out and I was trying to figure them out. That exclusion pushed me to try even harder to be INCLUDED. Because as a child, it doesn't feel good to be on the outside or to not understand the rules.

For much of my childhood, I was busy finding ways to step into the collective energy of the different groups, engaging in the third-dimensional reality of consciousness. I naturally wanted to be included in the activity of life going on around me.

So my thought processes and my learned behaviors were based on understanding the societal norms… and then conditioning myself to match them.

Once I was accepted into the group of friends and had people I could chat with, eat lunch with, hang out on the playground with, sit in class with, go play after school with… then I wanted to stay in that safe space. So I didn't push against those limitations. I stayed within the fence. Just like a sheep, I stayed within the fence line to be a part of the flock.

As a child, that was my Soul teaching me, showing me how necessary it can feel for survival to understand all of these societal rules. How we find ways to be included and protected.

I have lived this reality also in past lives, where being included in the group IS the only way that you survive. Everyone has a skill, a trade, a gift that they bring to the group and all of those individuals working together then allows for everyone's needs to be met. This was especially true before money became the currency – when your gift, your energy, your skill was your currency. Everyone had something unique that they would bring to the collective group to take care of each other.

If you dared to stand up and argue with the different gifts of each person or the different skills that each brings, or perhaps put your gift down and say *"I don't want to do this service anymore, I'm tired! I don't want to be a part of the collective,"* then you could get excluded from that group.

In the third dimensional reality, when you're excluded from the group, for most of our early lifetimes, that meant you had no food, support, clothing, housing or relationships. You were literally kicked out to survive on your own. And surviving on your own would often mean death because there was no support. If you laid down to rest at night, for example, and there was no-one to watch or protect you and you happened to be in the middle of a forest, well you could be eaten or killed by animals. Seriously!

The third-dimensional reality was a tough experience for humanity for much of our planet's history.

We are more refined these days. We have more physical resources around us now which allows us to feel more independent. But the Soul still remembers those experiences and nudges us to continue to play it safe in order to survive emotionally.

Our ancestral lineage is handed down through our cells from one generation to the next – *follow the rules and stay safe by staying in the group.*

War has also proven to us time and again that when you rebel you often lose. And even when you do "win" a war, what is the cost to humanity in the loss of lives and the destruction of property or to the safety, security, or steadiness that humans feel? War disrupts all of that. It throws security up in the air and messes with everything. And when all of the pieces land back on the ground again at the end of a war, they are never the same. Life is never the same.

In the third dimension, our ancestors have passed us these genetic codes, these truths because they've experienced them. They've handed us these truths and told us to stay safe, protect each other, and allow these mantras or belief systems to guide us so that we don't have to go through the pain that they had to before us.

Over time, as more Souls incarnate into our world, accepting these genetic codes, the energy field is becoming ever denser from the fear and blocked emotions being held inside our human bodies. Fear has become stronger and tighter in our physical systems.

None of this process has been wrong, though!

In the feeling of the fear, it offers us the opportunity to strengthen our resolve to create something different.

MORE gets created through contrast.

When people get frustrated with density, limitation, being told no and then feeling the resulting unresolved anger, disappointment, or powerlessness... the uprising of emotion inside can motivate them to break out of the mold and create something new.

That has been the intention for this planet: to allow space for creativity to flourish; for desire to expand; for new to be created. With every limitation, there exists the possibility to break through it and create something new and different.

From the beginning of time, the beginning of humanity on this planet, there have been individuals, Souls who have come to show other ways. To help nudge the general population. To create a spark of desire to create something new. They have come to help push humanity through to the next level.

And that has happened.

It has happened every time.

The higher dimensions have always existed. There have always been Souls who have agreed to come in and hold that higher vibration, hold that higher understanding of consciousness, love, and connection. And inspire more people to move towards that higher dimension.

But when you're the average Soul-human in the third-dimensional "reality" and everyone is telling you to follow the rules... often that dense reality is what your Soul experiences for many, many lifetimes.

> **From the Beginning of Humanity**
>
> **There has always been the Possibility**
>
> **Of a Different Experience**
>
> **Being Created on Earth.**

But as we are playing with time, space and the density of matter, the joy is in the contrast.

The joy is in understanding the limitations of the third dimension and feeling the heaviness of all of it. Having a human incarnation and feeling the frustration of not understanding or remembering the greatness of the Soul.

And then transitioning back to being a Soul again and going *"Oh, man! How did I not understand that?! How did I not see that?! How can it be so dense to be a human?"*

So then we come back into another incarnation with higher expectations and bigger goals, convinced that this time we're going to remember what it's like to be in the higher dimension and how awesome we are as Souls! We land back in the human body and find that it's the same density, the same heaviness, and the same contrast. *Uggghhh...*

And we transition back into the non-physical Soul again, saying *"Awww, no, I forgot again?!"*

Then back to another human incarnation where we don't get done what we think we're going to get done... and then we're back to being a Soul again, going *"Awww, how did I forget?!"*

> SOUND HEALING INTEGRATION:
> Avicii
> *"Wake Me Up"*

So there's this exciting, beautiful, powerful loop – Soul to human, human to Soul, Soul to human, human to Soul... And it's just Extraordinary!

It's.

Just.

Extraordinary!!

None of this has been wrong.

There's such an easy way that we typically tend to judge ourselves. We say *"Oh, here I am back in this limited third dimension. Again. I've never been able to make it to a higher dimension, why am I not in fourth or fifth?"*

No... it's the perfection of consciousness.

In human incarnations, every time you come in and have this physical experience, you become MORE. You are more than you were before you entered the human experience.

Your Soul expands.

Every incarnation is such a huge stretch for a Soul. To take on physical form, to play with aligning the physical and spiritual, working WITH the brain, WITH consciousness, holding thought, holding ideas, allowing creativity to move through and spark something within us – it is an incredible process!

Becoming a human ... Soul. Spiritual taking on human form is an incredible process.

Every single lifetime is a gift.

Every single lifetime matters.

Every Soul that comes and plays with humanity expands the entire collective energy of humanity. This is why our Earth's population is so dense now.

There's an excitement, a huge expansive ripple of energy that has been moving through our Universe because THIS planet, this Gaia offers such an incubation for consciousness to expand. Souls are drawn here to have the physical human experience, knowing it's going to be difficult, knowing they're going to scratch their heads and ask *"What am I doing here?!" Why am I even choosing this, what was I thinking?!"*

Yet, there still is this draw, this pull to come here and experience it.

To play, to delight in the physical form.

And so more and more Souls have been birthed into existence because this desire is so powerful, this creative energy is so powerful on Earth.

The number of stories, bodies, and ideas that need to exist to meet the excitement and the demand of Souls who want to come here – it just keeps expanding.

SLOWING DOWN

Now we have reached this point in humanity, this place here on Earth, where the energy, the heart, the consciousness that is our incubator, Gaia, is maximized.

Our planet is reaching the limitations of time, space, and the density of matter. Earth itself is reaching the limitations of what we created at the very beginning. This co-creation of everyone being here is taxing, maximizing what Gaia can hold.

There is a collective agreement between Souls (and the humans they inhabit), Gaia (our planet), and all the energies that exist in the cosmos, to slow down this race of time. To slow down this intensity of energy and physical matter so that we can allow Gaia some space to clear the dense third-dimensional energy and shift the vibration of consciousness from third into fourth into fifth.

> **The Next Level of Evolution Is One where our Creative Space Can be More Deliberate.**

The density of the third dimension is destroying our Earth. The Universal draw of Souls to experience being in human form is impacting the natural rhythm and energetic heartbeat of this planet. Our planet is ready for a big exhale. Gaia needs to exhale third-dimensional energy and inhale the natural energy of the Universe, which is Love. The original Source energy of the Universe, which is Love and Creativity and ever-expanding Consciousness.

So, it's not that we have been doing it wrong. It's that we have reached the limitations of time, space, and the density of matter on this physical planet we call Gaia.

We are rapidly approaching that limitation. There is a collective agreement from all Souls, Source, and Gaia to slow it all down... and now come into alignment with the higher dimensions.

YOU CAN HEAL YOUR LIFE

By Louise L. Hay

Where do you begin this journey of better understanding the human incarnation? In your body, of course! The body is the vehicle, the vessel, the physical representation of your energy and Soul. Falling in love with your own body and marveling at the magic and power of what the body can do and create is such a gift!

I begin every spiritual journey with new clients by referencing this book. Now 90 years old, Ms. Hay generously shares her lifetime of wisdom, teaching us how to tune into the ways that emotions and energy get stuck in our body. And then providing amazing suggestions on what we can actually DO about it!

The basis of every "dis-ease" comes from our thoughts and beliefs, many of which are toxic for our body. To change your health – change your thoughts.

Many years ago as a Mama of two young children in daycare and school, this book became my go-to reference for every illness that would pop up in their little bodies. I would flip to the back of the book, scan the chart of illnesses and see what might be happening emotionally with them. This allowed our conversations to change and helped me feel more empowered in my communications with their doctors. Now, when my own body twinges, aches, or puts me down in my bed for a couple days, I understand where the emotional need to pause is stemming from and can shift it more easily by re-aligning my thoughts.

Thank you, thank you, thank you, Ms. Hay. xoxo

AFTERGLOW

As I end each chapter, I am including a brief story or quote from a Soul-human who is in the dimension being described at the time of writing this book and who generously offers his/her *"I'm Living it Now"* perspective for you.

For the third dimension, however, just turn on any news outlet and read the headlines to find example after example of Soul-humans who feel trapped by limitation and lack.

My hope is that because you are reading this book and have allowed yourself the space to explore a new perspective on consciousness that you have already or are in this moment beginning your own expansion.

SOUND HEALING INTEGRATION:
Cristina Aguilera
"Cruz"

Why?

Because it means that you are becoming MORE… and that is why we exist.

Vivienne Gerard

ONE DAY

4

FOURTH DIMENSION

"Bouncing"

Vivienne Gerard

FOURTH DIMENSION

When we are in the womb of our mother, we merge the Infinite Soul and a tiny human body into one combined energy in physical form. The consciousness that we bring with us is guiding the process and working with the energy of Mama to understand the Earth environment that the little baby will be stepping into when he/she is born.

It is a highly creative time for both Mama and baby... and all of it happens within nine months!

Then. We. Arrive.

SOUND HEALING INTEGRATION: Craig Pruess and Ananda "Devi Prayer"

We are born into the physical and the many Soul contracts we've made with our loved ones... the memories of past lifetimes... the gifts and purpose we bring into this lifetime...

ALL

ARE

FORGOTTEN!

What?!

Yes... this is the fun of human incarnation!

To begin again, over and over. Relearning the spiritual-physical dance.

Healing the places where our Souls got "stuck" or "wounded" in past incarnations.

Expanding our own Knowing through more experiences, more contrast, and more relationships.

So as you and I begin our journey together through the dimensions beyond the third-dimensional "reality," it feels important to remind you that **you already know** all that you're going to remember as you read this book. I am simply a guide, sharing My Soul Journey with you, trusting that it provides openings exactly as YOU need them, in the perfect timing for your Soul, and always with the greatest of Love.

SOUND HEALING INTEGRATION:

Snatam Kaur "Carry Me"

Your "work" is to allow your physical body to connect back in and re-align with your Infinite Soul…

… your ever-expanding consciousness.

So. Let's explore the Fourth Dimension!

The best way to describe it is a confusing shift of: *"I believe the world might be different than how I've always understood it to be. I believe things may work differently than I've always expected they may work. But I'm not sure. And, if this IS all true, I don't really know what to even do about it!"*

Perhaps in the past, you thought you were always a certain way, a certain size or personality, a certain image or archetype. Boxed in. Limited.

As you shift into the fourth dimension, you start stretching or expanding how you see yourself. A window opens (or maybe at first just the curtain covering that window opens!) and you can see that maybe things aren't always quite what you believed they were. What everyone had programmed and told you they would be.

If you are a person who built walls and limitations around yourself for much of your life, then your movement into the fourth dimension begins to show you that perhaps there's something more to you here in this lifetime. Perhaps your experiences could be different. Maybe the world is more amazing and this journey of life is more incredible than what you believe it has offered you so far.

There's an anticipation... a feeling of excitement, hope, and pleasure that expands within the physical body in this transitional time. Moments or interactions that leave you feeling a little fizzy, a little bubbly, like *"Woah, I didn't realize! And that's kind of exciting! And who knew it could be all that?!"* You start experiencing this feeling of being bigger than who you thought you always were.

BUT...

Then...

There's a contraction that comes in right as you're starting to be amazed at who you are becoming!

Ughhhhh!

Bumpy landing back into the "real world" through a fight with your partner or co-worker, an illness that has you feeling miserable, an unexpected financial stress. All kinds of limitations can show back up for the contraction!

In the fourth dimension, life feels very much as if you are a jellyfish moving through the water. As jellyfish move, their bodies contract in and expand out, go in and go out, in and out. They are moving through the water, perhaps with or without a clear understanding of where they are going next, moving and stretching through their space, breath by breath.

Expand and contract, expand and contract.

That is exactly what the fourth dimension feels like. You feel great for a moment, an hour, or a week and then you suddenly come crashing back into the limitations of the third's "reality" and you don't know if that new joy that you experienced was even true. And then you expand again, feeling the possibility of *"Woah, it could be different"* ... and then you contract back in again.

There's this emotional and spiritual movement that can feel a bit dizzying. A bit like a yo-yo.

A little exhausting when you're sitting in the middle of it.

> **SOUND HEALING INTEGRATION:**
> *Imagine Dragons "Friction"*

Confusing.

Disorienting.

In this space, you start to understand how limiting the world was in the way that you'd always viewed it. You go back and forth between hopeful, optimistic, excited and then uuggghhh... crashing down into reality. But this is exactly the process that needs to happen for third-dimensional energy to make its way out of your physical body and for your heart and your Soul to release that dimension and flow into a more expansive field.

So there's a shedding that happens when you shift dimensional levels. A shedding of the old, like a snakeskin, where the snake outgrows its skin and leaves that layer behind. It is the same snake the whole way through all of its transformations, through all of the times that it sheds its skin... it's the same snake, simply shedding its old layer to allow the new skin room to breathe. To allow the snake to grow bigger.

To expand its capacity.

It is the same for us with dimensions of consciousness.

As the spiritual and physical are shifting from the third dimension to the fourth dimension, there is a letting go, a releasing that happens physically and spiritually. The process looks different for everyone, depending on your stories, your beliefs, and the way that you see yourself.

For me, I felt confusion, anger, and disappointment during my shedding of the layers. I could feel the expectations I held for others not being met and then how I personalized that as MY own limitations. I believed it was my fault that people weren't able to meet me or see me or understand me. When really, it was simply that I was stretching and growing. I had expanded past the limitations of some of those old relationships, jobs, projects and belief systems.

So where I took it personally and thought someone was judging me or something was wrong with me or lacking in me, it was actually that my internal capacity had expanded and the flow of energy between me and those things that I used to engage with had shifted.

During these times of expansion, it might feel like you have "outgrown" a relationship, but that subtly implies a feeling of superiority or a sense of leaving others behind.

Every Soul has their own timing, their own journey.

Every Soul has lessons that they are working on as they incarnate. And so every expansion that happens through your heart and your spirit is in the perfect timing for you.

There is no race.

No getting ahead of someone else. Or leaving someone behind. Or competing or challenging against another.

It isn't that at all.

Sometimes we might have Souls who play a role in motivating us in our lives. Or who, through contrast, push us to expand so that we leap into whatever the next level is. But it's never because there's some race between Souls to get to some imaginary finish line faster than another. At a Soul level, every single Soul is here to support the other, whether we do it through walking alongside someone or through showing contrast, helping ourselves and others to release old energies.

> *SOUND HEALING INTEGRATION:*
> *U2*
> *"Song for Someone"*

> **Whichever Way We Play,**
> **The Point of the Journey Always**
> **Is to Support and Expand**
> **Every Soul**
> **Into More Love.**

Every Soul.

And so if we honor the path of each individual Soul as perfect, as already complete and whole, then there is no lack or disappointment or judgment that needs to last. It can just be feeling the contrast and whatever it brings up in us, moving through it, expanding, then moving into whatever our next adventure or learning is that we're doing.

And then loving the other exactly where they are.

Which feels important... and yet is not always so easy to

do as we're transitioning through all of these dimensional changes, right?!

Knowing what the highest potential could be and simultaneously being stuck in the old patterns.

Bouncing.

MY TRANSITION TO 4TH

My expansion into fourth was a physical shift, an energetic shift, a spiritual shift. It felt like the veils were becoming thinner all around me. Doors were creaking open a bit. I couldn't quite tell what was on the other side or what might be coming through. I just knew that something in me was becoming more certain. Something was clearer than it had been before.

And it was FUN!

It felt delightful! It felt exciting to trust myself in that way.

And... then. BUMP!

I would get pulled back into the old stories and have to dig through the confusion to find clarity again.

An example feels like it would be useful here.

My shift to the fourth dimension started in the summer of 2015. At the time, I was consulting with another coach through her business, building a client base and expanding the ways I used energy in my work. As I was bouncing around in the fourth dimension, I would get hurt and disappointed when I felt like I wasn't been seen or accepted for who I was in my gifts.

Things felt very confusing as changes were constantly

and simultaneously happening in my own self-growth, in my coaching work with clients, and in my relationship with my partner in the business. Differences were coming up quickly to be examined in all areas. The speed of the changes (both business and personal) felt scary to me.

If you had met me then, I would have told you with total conviction that I felt sad and hurt because I wasn't being loved or accepted for who I was. That my relationship with my business partner (and friend) was falling apart because I wasn't being valued. My old stories of fear about not being included in the tribe were coming up powerfully so that I could explore them. *Ouch!*

AND... then I could finally start healing and releasing those old stories.

With perspective, further down the road, what I know for sure is that our Souls already had both of us on a path that was for our highest good... which would mean separating to allow space for each of us to grow further and to expand into our gifts individually in richer and fuller ways.

But in the process, as it's unfolding, it feels very confusing. Frustrating. Overwhelming.

I can see now for myself that the catalyst for my change was to see the situation as black and white, believing that I was right and she was wrong... which would then give me the strength to leave. The strength to hold my ground. To claim my space. Which was a huge shift from the third-dimensional version of me who might never have had the courage to make such a big change and step out on my own.

The judgments I made gave me permission to leave the flock. To make a dramatic change. A change that was guided by my Soul to help me continue expanding consciousness.

ONE DAY

To become more.
Always More.

NAVIGATING THIS SHIFT

So how do we navigate this bouncing arena of the fourth dimension?

My best advice is to go slowly at this time, if possible. To be patient and kind with yourself. To forgive yourself for not always being clear or having it all figured out.

To talk things through with people you trust and who you know love you so that you don't get all clouded and confused in your own head space.

As consciousness expands, we are continually being offered the opportunity to tune into the quieter voice inside each of us. We begin learning how to decipher our own unique Soul voice from the chaos and the busyness of all the voices that go on around us, in our heads, and in our physical world.

SOUND HEALING INTEGRATION: My Soul Journey "Changing the Story"

We have so much energy and information coming towards us in all moments in this evolving age of technology. It feels like there's a barrage of information that's constantly coming our way!

Now is a time to find whatever processes or ways you can to turn down the world's density and the third-dimensional limitations and chatter. So that you can find and get clearer and clearer on what YOUR Soul is saying to you, what your Soul is guiding you towards next.

Because ultimately, every Soul in their expansion is being guided forward through the dimensions of consciousness.

Like a never-ending train track.

You're going from fourth to fifth to sixth to seventh – it's forward, it's always expanding into MORE.

If we're all being guided into our own unique ways of being more, feeling more and holding more, then each person, each Soul needs to identify what their train track, their path looks like because it will be different from everyone else's. And it's hard to know what that path or way is going to look like if you're overwhelmed with the noise and voices of everyone around you.

Start creating a structured practice where you have quiet time. Where there is room for your voice to whisper to you.

Whether it's through meditation, exercise, prayer, dance, walking, lying in bed for an extra five or ten minutes in the morning, allowing your mind to just wander and your Soul to inform you.

SOUND HEALING INTEGRATION:

Caspian "Waking Season"

Build a practice that allows you to tune into yourself in new ways.

To feel the emotions that want to come up. To remember the stories that need space to process. So that they can move. Often it's not even a 'digging into old things' that has to be done. It's simply allowing room for the memories to come up, be lightly touched and felt, and then move through. That's often enough. And if it feels like more digging is needed at times, get the coaching support you need to heal.

The important piece is to create the practice, structure, and the discipline in your routine so that you can expand your heart... you can breathe into this fourth dimension. And not feel overwhelmed or intimidated by it. It can just be this easy, graceful movement forward and through, a releasing of any old stories, old beliefs, and old heaviness.

In the fourth dimension, you may start experiencing a pull or a call towards activities that you've never been interested in before. That make no sense to the people around you!

The Soul is so wise.

It will always pull towards us what will most serve.

The Soul will plant that perfect opportunity for growth right in front of us.

And if we trust what the signs are... if we listen when we feel the jump in our heart when something shows up that feels absolutely perfect and completely terrifying... if we trust that... if we have enough quiet external space to feel the internal pulse giving a little pitter-patter beat in a new way... if we trust that and follow it, then our Soul is going to guide us to exactly where we need to be, with exactly the next step that would most serve us.

And it will be different for everyone.

For me, first, it was music.

That summer of 2015, I was gifted with a powerful sound healing with a shaman. It was the first time I'd ever experienced a ceremony guided by sound. This beautiful ancient healer was playing music in our small gathering with his indigenous, handmade instruments and then adding in modern music

SOUND HEALING INTEGRATION:
Rafael Bejarano
"Ofrende a la Madre Tierra"

from his phone. Many were songs and artists I didn't know, musicians I wasn't familiar with, new kinds of meditation or shamanic music.

I was entranced!!

So I started filling up the playlist of my own phone. I would play music when I ran each morning, when I was home by myself working, when I was in the car with my family and when I was laying by the pool meditating.

I would play all of these different pieces of music and feel the activation of something shifting inside of me. Knowing that I was hearing sounds I had loved before in other lifetimes... and feeling the memories of those lifetimes stirring.

For some of the music, there was just a calm, settling feeling in my heart or my stomach. I could feel my whole body grounding energetically and connecting with the Earth as the songs played. I was feeling energy moving through me in different ways as the music guided me. It would show me a new pathway.

Music would quiet the chatter in my mind and allow me to experience the space where my Soul could just float, my Soul could play, could whisper to me.

Meditation.... I started meditating more. I was also journaling more during this phase.

I was accessing memories from my past lives. A doorway opened for me that summer, allowing me to feel Truth across time and space. I would have shivers or chills move through my body when I knew I was tapping into memories from other lifetimes for myself, my clients, and my friends.

I developed a trust of my body in a whole new way through muscle testing.

Feeling Truth as a physical knowing.

I would hold my hand out, press one finger against the other, speak a statement and KNOW in every cell in my body that what I was saying was my Truth – or clearly not my Truth. It was a significant change for me to be so certain in my body after a lifetime of not paying attention to my own body!

SOUND HEALING INTEGRATION:

My Soul Journey "Muscle Testing" video

This was a shift from handing my power over to other people for validation and instead fully trusting myself.

That summer and fall I could feel a new certainty landing within myself. *"I know this is true. I don't need anyone else to confirm this. My body and my soul and my heart are telling me yes. And I trust this so completely."*

ENERGY PLAY

As the body and Soul are coming more into alignment, grounding energetically is an important tool. To clarify, it's not that you're grounding into the third dimension and staying rooted in that reality. No, instead you are practicing grounding your own energy into your own physical body.

You're landing all of your energy in You.

From there, you can really play with expanding and contracting and it doesn't make you as wobbly. The yo-yo feeling doesn't throw you off balance as much.

If you are new to energy work, energetic grounding is a simple practice to include in your daily activities *(and the next Sound Healing suggestion is a powerful resource!).*

Picture your physical body as a tree and then visualize yourself growing roots deep down into the earth underneath your feet.

Feel the earth's rich soil holding you firmly in place, just like a tree that has a strong root system underneath the ground. If it's helpful, picture the tallest Redwood in a California forest or the oldest Sycamore or Oak tree and match your strength and stability to that mental image.

> SOUND HEALING INTEGRATION:
> Liquid Bloom
> "Roots of the Earth"

"Rooting in" and anchoring your attention into each moment is a powerful way to move through this bouncing phase quickly.

The fourth-dimensional shift is a good time for quiet space, reflection, contemplation, meditation – all of those practices that can support you grounding your energy IN-to your body, anchoring IN-to what is coming through next.

Which is likely a little bit more of that push-pull feeling!

Up-down, backwards-forwards, yo-yo. There's a lot moving in the fourth dimension as you clear out so many of the old stories in your life.

For some people, this dimensional shift can be really brief. Just a few weeks or a month or two. For other people, it could be a year, two years, or many years.

I believe now, though, with the way that the planet is shifting, people will not be spending many years in the fourth dimension anymore. The movement will be faster through these levels because there are such higher levels of light and energy entering our Earth, which increase the feeling of being propelled forward.

CHAKRAS FOR BEGINNERS

By David Pond

For many of us, this idea of chakras or energy centers can feel mysterious – perhaps even intimidating to begin exploring. And yet we know or can sense that we feel stuck or blocked inside and we're not sure how to shift what doesn't even have a physical form.

Mr. Pond *"shows you how to align your energy using the body's chakra system so you can achieve balance from the inside out. Through practical activities, meditations, and powerful techniques, you'll work with each of your seven chakras to overcome imbalances and advance on your spiritual path."* Do not be fooled by the title that it is only for beginners – he provides a wealth of information to assist anyone interested in better understanding how to feel energy, balancing and activating the chakras.

I found this book when I was beginning my journey as a coach and healer. While I had studied chakras and the flow of energy for several years, the simple ways that the author shared his wisdom just landed solidly in me. Probably half of my copy is underlined, with notes everywhere!

Here's an example in the Preface of why I trust Mr. Pond… *"I do not present these ideas as absolute truth, instead they are 'works in progress,' and when the reader has a different experience than I present, I encourage you to go with your personal truth. That is what it is all about: accessing your direct personal experience of the various centers of consciousness."*

Yes, indeed. Xoxo

Even though perhaps you're not feeling quite physically or emotionally ready for changes, your Soul always knows when you're ready to expand, which is why you step into that space.

Your Soul is guiding you into the next level of awareness.

So it really is about Trust.

Trust what shows up. Follow the signs. Follow the guidance. ALLOW yourself to be guided. Allow yourself to believe that everything that you're sensing IS possible.

If you see it, if you feel it, if you hold the vibration of it inside your Soul and anchor that into your physical body, your physical time, your physical life... there's no way you can't reach that next space.

The only unknown is how long it will take.

And that really depends on how strong your faith is in yourself.

How strong your belief is in what you're seeing for yourself.

SOUND HEALING INTEGRATION:
Temper Trap "Alive"

How strong your desire is to expand.

How in touch you are with your feelings. If you can allow yourself to feel the pleasure, the joy, the delight, and then hold that vibration as you move forward.

Because you can't go backward in dimensions. Once you complete one level and expand into the next, you don't contract all the way back down again.

You can't be LESS conscious than you were before. You're only expanding into MORE consciousness. More awareness. More understanding. You don't go backward.

And so the density of the third dimension starts to shed like a snakeskin. And that new, trembly, unsure, not quite formed fourth-dimensional version of you has room to be created.

It is an incredible process, playing with consciousness in this way. The reverence, the kindness, and gentleness that you show yourself makes such a difference.

Deep breath.

As we prepare to leave the fourth dimension and step into the fifth, allow Breath to carry you through the shift.

In yoga, we are guided to align with breath and trust that it will carry us through any position that is stretching our physical bodies.

SOUND HEALING INTEGRATION:
MSJ YouTube "Purifying Breath Meditation"

To *Lean Into* the posture and feel each breath coming in and then gently leaving our bodies.

It is the same for these shifts of consciousness.

Take a moment to catch and then release your breath... feel the movement of your breath... and trust the certainty of more breath always arriving in the next moment.

All is well.

AFTERGLOW

Remember when I mentioned that you might feel pulled towards new activities that make no sense to the people around you?

One of my clients, Jen, was pulled towards pole dancing in her fourth dimensional transition, something that perhaps she'd always been curious about but had never had the courage to try.

She is a Ring Soul Filter *(more on the Soul Filters in the Sixth Dimension!)*, which is very much about fun and body. So it would make sense that she was pulled towards something that would help her tune into her body, listen to the gentle nuances of what her body was inviting her to do and move and feel, teaching her how to run energy through her body in ways she didn't know before.

This new call to pole dancing gave her a way to play with all that was shifting inside of her. It offered her a safe place where she could tune out the busyness of the world around and hear her own Soul whispers, her own body's tenderness and strength, the desire of her body to play and delight in sensation. She listened and then created a space for herself to have that creative time which then guided her into more clarity about next steps for her relationships and career.

It feels important as we wrap up this phase of "bouncing" to offer the confirmation of a gentle landing space in the fifth dimension through Jen's example.

When I met Jen three years ago, she was a very busy and successful corporate manager with a full family life. And she could feel that she was shifting, but didn't know where her path was taking her.

She transitioned into the fourth dimension when she left her full time job to start a coaching business and work from home. *YIKES!* Talk about leaving the density of the third dimension and stepping into the unknown!

She bounced in the fourth dimension for almost a year, going through beautiful shifts in many of the relationships in her life as she released old patterns and stories.

Expanding and stretching – and then bumping roughly back down into the old density and confusion.

Up again, down again.

And then one night just a couple months ago, she posted a branded inspirational photo on Facebook with an amazing quote that completely captured who she was becoming!

I texted her as soon as I saw it, with these exact words: *"JEN!!!! You just nailed it, my Love!!!! YES, YES, YES! You are ON your path… Keep the energy flowing, it is powerful!"*

She landed.

…

Let's go explore Fifth!

Vivienne Gerard

5

FIFTH DIMENSION

"Explore"

Vivienne Gerard

FIFTH DIMENSION

It's funny, as I was recording the audio for this section of the book, my one-year-old puppy, Star, kept whining at the front door, wanting to go out and just looking at the door – why is it still closed? I could almost imagine his thoughts of, *"Wait, wait, wait... I'm tired of waiting! Why do I still have to wait?!"*

Which is exactly what it feels like when you are in fourth, knowing there is something *right there*. If you could only remember, feel it, sense it. You're pacing around like my puppy was doing - waiting, waiting, waiting for someone to open the door.

And then it just...

...it just suddenly opens one day.

That is what it feels like with the fifth dimension.

Just all of a sudden, consciousness gracefully expands and something shifts inside of you. Inside of your heart. And suddenly you just KNOW that life is good. You know that everything is going to work out for your higher purpose.

You know that you ARE Love.

> **You have Always Been Love.**

Everyone you know is Love. But you didn't believe it or

allow it to go all the way through your body in the way that it does when you step into the fifth dimension.

And it does feel like a "stepping into." There's a conscious choice that happens when you step into the fifth dimension of *"I claim it for myself. I know this to be true."* There's a feeling of being at a crossroads, a threshold, and you either are going to stay where you are or now choose to go left or right or straight ahead.

Which way to go? The fifth-dimensional shift is *"I'm choosing my HIGHEST path. I'm choosing my highest purpose."*

Because the momentum of life, of consciousness, will eventually keep moving you forward. You'll never be less than. But when you choose to deliberately step into this next dimension of energy, of thought, of creation, it's with a knowing that you have something unique to bring to the world that nobody else does in your way.

That you as a Soul have a specific ability or gift or magic that you agreed to share with humanity. And you're ready to start exploring what that is... Now.

And so saying yes to the fifth dimension, choosing the new path that looks really scary will completely thrill you and terrify you all at the same time.

That **choice** is what activates the consciousness shift.

For me it was the choice to leave the coaching partnership that wasn't serving me anymore, that was holding me back from what I knew I could bring forward in my gifts. The choice to step into my own business, step into my own way of doing my coaching work – that **choice** was my activation into fifth.

SOUND HEALING INTEGRATION:

Imagine Dragons *"It's Time"*

Despite all of the internal and external resistance, I said, *"Yes, I'm doing this thing that feels risky and crazy. And I also know it's in my highest purpose to find out what my deepest work looks like next."*

That choice was an activation.

That's why I use the words "stepping into." It is a step across, a step forward, a step into the next level of understanding. It isn't a default of *"I just happened to be in fifth, I just happened to choose this path."*

It's an active, conscious choice.

When that happens, it feels a bit like when you step from a rocking boat onto solid ground. It takes a while to find your land legs. There's a shifting from one platform to another platform – from one dimension to another dimension.

The third dimension has probably felt really stable and predictable for years. Even though it's heavy and dense, it is still familar. Then the fourth dimension has felt like a yo-yo: up into the possibilities and then back down to Earth, up and back down to Earth, bouncing… until you finally are ready to shift again.

When you step into the fifth dimension, it can still feel a bit wobbly as you get used to the changes. You know something is different inside your heart, inside your Soul. But your physical body is going *"Woah – what does this mean? What is happening? Why is this going on?"*

It is a time of letting go of old attachments. Letting go of those things that you experienced in a state of fear in the third dimension. There is a full release that happens throughout the fifth dimension of those old ways, old beliefs, and old stories.

So, naturally, relationships begin to feel rocky or feel a little different.

I noticed this happening especially in my own parent-child relationships. For me, with my parents, it was a time of drawing back into my own space, not being as communicative as I had been with them on a regular basis.

Needing to explore spiritually, *"Who am I as an individual, not just as the daughter of Tom and Cynthia? Who am I, Vivienne? Completely separate from all of the old definitions of who I have been before."*

What it looked like in the activity of my life was less time with my parents, fewer interactions. Not because they did something wrong or because I didn't love them anymore, but because I needed that cocoon, that internal space to figure out who I am, separate from them.

It was also a time of more independence within my immediate family of my husband and children. It was a time for me to claim, *"This is how I want my schedule to look. How I want my business to run. These are the words I choose to use to describe myself. These are the images that align with how I see energy, how I see life, how I see my gifts."* Those were all of MY identifications being created in a physical manner, playing out through the establishing of my business.

If your activation to the fifth dimension is also through the separation of a relationship and claiming of your own space, you might be exploring different aspects of individuality.

For example, if you choose to separate from your roommate or partner and need to move - where do you actually want to live? What type of home do YOU prefer? What furniture would you use to decorate your home? What types of food do you actually enjoy cooking? Do you even enjoy cooking?!

We are redefining who we know ourselves to be.

It can feel confusing to those people with whom you are in close relationship if you become more internal. It can feel to them like you don't want to be around them, or there's something wrong with them and that's why you're not hanging out as often.

But it's really so much about your own internal journey. Your own internal sorting through things. Deciding *"is this belief I've always had about myself... is it is even true, or is it just what I inherited from what people had always told me to be true?"*

One of the identifications that I played with all of last year was the contrast or balance of my internal strengths of Love and Spirit. For much of my life, I've seen myself as being very heart-centered and flowing so much love to everyone. And while that is true, there is also this HUGE Spirit side of me, this old Soul that sees and knows things. When I have identified myself so strongly with *"love, love, love, love, heart, heart, heart, heart..."* there isn't always enough room for the Spirit side to step in and offer, *"But I SEE and I know and I trust and I can guide."* Finding ways to allow both to flow through and merge in an even more empowered way was fascinating!

This deep identifying and re-evaluating of Self - it is an incredible time, an incredible process, and unfolding that happens. It can feel scary... or you can look at it as an adventure, as a time of the most amazing discovery of Self.

SOUND HEALING INTEGRATION:

Bachan Kaur
"Forgiveness"

This remembering of your Soul and other lifetimes you have lived, other projects you have been pulled towards, the gifts that you know intuitively in your Soul... all have space to come out when you create a little cocoon for self-discovery.

MY TRANSITION TO 5TH

I shifted into the fifth dimension in October of 2015, followed through on my choice to leave my friend and business partner in November, and then really just huddled into myself for the next month. That December was a beautiful healing time for me, sitting quietly with myself, journaling, talking to friends, meditating, sleeping, still doing my work with my clients, but mostly a LOT of introspection time.

In the beginning of the New Year, I set the intention that I would meditate every day for an hour. So for those first four or five months of 2016, I was just sitting quietly every morning, meditating and questioning, *"What are my gifts? What are the things I love to do? Not based on what everyone has told me to be true about myself, but what do I feel, what do I know to be true about how I like to communicate? What would I say to clients if I was fully trusting my own intuition? What tools are natural for me to use in my coaching work?"*

It was an amazing time!

My meditations changed, daily. The information that was starting to come through would arrive as I was ready for it.

For example, I would get a nudge to create a meditation about breathing. So I created Purifying Breath, a 40-minute download from Source that flowed through on my forty-fifth birthday.

And then by March, I was guided towards practicing 30 Days of Meditation by showing up each day in front of my computer with my microphone, just recording whatever came through! Thirty days for 10, 15, or 30 minutes each time, I would sit and tune in to simply flow through whatever energy wanted to move. And magic happened! Every time.

All of this creative information that I hadn't accessed before – I had time and space to explore it in the fifth dimension. I trusted that I was safe. I had physical support around me with my husband, my clients, my friends, my children, my family. And so there was a safe, quiet space for me to go IN.

I also needed more sleep as all of this was changing so quickly. I didn't want a full, busy schedule so I slowed my life down. I wanted time to meditate and feel into whatever was moving inside of me. I wanted the slower pace.

But I also started running a lot physically, every day, to help move all of this new energy through my body.

Music was still guiding me, and I started expanding my library of music, listening to the lyrics of the songs. That was when I surrendered to Source being the guide on my playlist. I just handed it over! I would hit shuffle on my phone as I started my run and allow Source to move through technology and play music to me, sing the songs. And of course, it was always perfect. The song I needed came right through, each day, with wisdom to help me resolve questions about work or relationships.

And mmm, yes – the sunshine! I noticed that I really craved LIGHT at that time. I wanted to be in the sun more than I had ever remembered needing it before.

> *SOUND HEALING INTEGRATION:*
> *Donna DeLory*
> *"In The Sun"*

I was becoming more present in my own life. With myself and with others.

I was SLOWING DOWN.

NAVIGATING THIS SHIFT

This is my greatest recommendation to anyone finding themselves now in the fifth dimension:

Slow down the pace of your life in the physical.

Slow down how much you're doing and how many people you're doing it with and create a quiet mental space where you can pause the chatter of life, of activities, of deadlines, of tasks, of busyness.

Sit quietly with your Soul.

Make that a daily practice. A half hour, an hour if you can do it. Trust. Even if you're sitting there for a few days or a week or two and nothing comes through, and you're frustrated because you're sitting, you're doing what you said you would do... and nothing is happening.

Give your body, your Soul, your Spirit a little time and space to come into alignment. Perhaps use guided meditations at first if the quiet is too intense. Listen to a guided meditation for fifteen minutes and then sit for another 15 or 20, just quietly, and allow the thoughts to move through.

Sit in nature.

Just watch. Watch the birds. Watch the trees. Watch the waves if you're lucky enough to be by the ocean! Watch the clouds. Lay in a field and watch the clouds.

Allow yourself to just be present. To feel any emotion that is moving through.

This is usually when your subconscious is going to bring forward the things that need to be looked at and released or healed. So you may lay there for five or ten minutes, feeling peaceful, and then suddenly there's an image of a person that used to bully you or that you got into a fight with when you were 5 or 10 years old. Just sit there and allow the memory to gently have space. Feel the emotions that come up from that experience. And then use your breath. Breathe the emotions out, run that energy down to your feet and release it into the Earth.

Set up these cocoons, these pockets of time and space where you can just allow Life to be an experience that you have had and are still having now. Without judging it or evaluating if you did it right or wrong or if that person was good or bad.

Just let it be emotions that move through. And again if you need more support, talk to a friend, a coach, or your spiritual guide. If it feels too heavy or dense to navigate, or if your emotions feel too overwhelming, get support.

SOUND HEALING INTEGRATION:
My Soul Journey
"Energy Flowing"

This space in the fifth dimension is a time for all of those old attachments to unravel. Those cords that have had you wrapped up, tied up, and believing all of these old things to be true, you're allowing space for that to unwind. So it can look and feel messy!

It is a time of healing for your Soul.

The fifth dimension is also an activation of the throat, the fifth chakra energetically. Using your voice and activating the unique sound that is your identification in this lifetime, in this body, in this moment.

In this self-discovery phase, there are expressions that your throat chakra will want to share. Perhaps start by sharing those with people you trust and love, who can receive them and reflect gently back to you, supporting you as emotions are coming up.

As you get clearer in the fifth dimension, you move towards this space of wanting to express your throat chakra in louder ways. So you start to find these opportunities – or they will find their way towards you – where you can express your beliefs, your emotions, your stories, and your knowing from this lifetime and all lifetimes. You can begin expressing that truth OUT in small groups if that feels right to you first, and then bigger groups.

The stronger, the more solid you become as you move through the fifth dimension, the more your voice will resonate outwards to other people. The more impact your throat chakra can have.

SOUND HEALING INTEGRATION:
Katy Perry "Roar"

This is also an important time to ground your energy, which allows you to feel solid in your body and solid in this moment. To feel connected to the Earth, trusting that what is coming through serves you *and* serves all of humanity.

The fifth dimension is a beautiful place to play and explore and try out new things. Especially if you're not attached to the outcome.

For me, I was playing with all different ways to teach meditation. And then exploring how I felt as I was sharing that gift; how it was being received by others; where there were needs that weren't being met in the collective energy of the world.

It can be a fascinating time!

INSPIRED GUIDANCE

It also feels like in the fifth dimension there is access to a higher collective field of consciousness that you can't quite feel in the third and fourth dimensions.

For example, I found clarity on who my immediate Soul guides were... my spirit guides who were actively working with me. Then it was amazing to trust the messages that they would send me. To sit in my meditation and hear the energetic voices, the words, the guidance that they were offering. My journal became filled with notes, messages from what some might call "the other side," but what I call simply Energy, Love, or Consciousness. These messages would clarify wisdom for me and then that information would guide my next steps.

SOUND HEALING INTEGRATION:

Ford Atlantic
"Let your heart hold fast"

Trusting and acting on your intuition is a BIG part of the growth in the fifth dimension.

Can you receive a message from your guides, feel the specific next steps from the collective consciousness that aligns us with Source, and then act on it?

The more that you act on that pure guidance... the more guidance can come through behind it. Because the trust is being built – within yourself and around you energetically. The more you trust your intuition, the more you receive support. The more you trust that support, the more support you receive – it just keeps growing!

And so you eventually feel like you are just floating downstream. There's no swimming against the current or work or effort that needs to happen.

There is just this pure, clear guidance and you're surrendering to it, over and over and over again. Your life is just flowing and aligning in ways that you couldn't have created.

It is a really playful, fun, delightful time!

THE SURRENDER EXPERIMENT

By Michael Singer

Okay – the concept behind this one is a doozy and it rocked my world in the best of ways! I found SUCH power in witnessing Mr. Singer's journey as he *"tells the extraordinary story of what happened when, after a deep spiritual awakening, he decided to let go of his personal preferences and simply let life call the shots."*

He said YES to whatever showed up in his life. Not *"maybe, or next time, or only if these conditions are met"* – he said yes every time to every situation. And the path he was taken down unexpectedly and beautifully offered him a *"journey into life's perfection."*

I read this book when I was resisting making changes in my life and I remember being absolutely amazed that Mr. Singer literally said yes to every single thing. I wouldn't make the same leap to always saying yes, but I would remember his trust in life in moments when I had to choose which way to go, and I would pause... center... breathe... and consider what a YES would mean in that moment. If I could expand my perspective to see life through a wider lens, the choice was clearer.

Mr. Singer offers this beautiful description of a healing center that came from one of his YES choices: *"This temple sat on the planet Earth, a tiny ball spinning through the vast darkness of empty space. It spun around one star, of which there were billions in our galaxy alone. This temple was universal in its embrace of all the religions, and it was universal in its embrace of the universe itself. Thus it came to be called – Temple of The Universe."*

A tiny taste of the gift of this book! xoxo

ONE DAY

How long does it last?

Until you are ready for the next shift!

For me, the fifth dimension lasted from October 2015 until June 2016. But there's no set time frame for any person to follow a certain pattern. Your Soul knows when you are ready to expand.

For those nine months, I was exploring, detaching, releasing what I had always believed must be true about life, work, jobs, businesses, client-coach relationships, money, time, health. There was so much letting go happening.

I felt like I was pushing the boundaries of my comfort zone so much during this time. I set up my own website, started a YouTube channel to host my new recorded meditations, began writing articles, hosting retreats at my home... There was so much expansion happening and I just trusted how I was being guided. I had majored in business in college and worked for several successful businesses in my career, so this unknown "Operating Plan" didn't make any logical sense! But I trusted.

I kept following what I was being pulled towards.

I absolutely was (and still am) being Divinely supported through the whole process. The income I needed would come right when I needed it. The work I needed would be teaching me exactly what I needed to be learning in that moment. There really was this beautiful alignment and flow that was happening in all areas of my life as I learned to pay attention to my own inner voice and the wisdom of my guides.

I became more transparent with my beliefs and the kind of healing work I wanted to do. For me, so much of this time was about becoming more transparent. Which can feel scary and also so, so exciting!

The possibilities feel wide open for who you can be, how you can look, what you can share of your Truth...

The next shift from fifth to sixth is the claiming of what your unique, individual work is that you're here to do in this lifetime. One of many Soul gifts you bring with you, but the claiming of the first, main thing.

When you claim it, there's this *whhhhooooowwwwww* as you move into the next dimension. It's so good!

So good!

AFTERGLOW

One of my client-friends *(who taught me SO much when I was really learning how fun and FAST this energy work could be!)* referred her partner to me after a sudden death in his family. And so I was introduced to Mike, who felt like an old friend from our very first conversation.

We had layers of grief and family chaos to work through in the density of his third dimensional reality – and it took a lot of patience and commitment on his part to keep coming back to look at those painful stories. But something shifted after five months of regular sessions and it was immediately noticeable.

He had moved into fourth!

I shared with him the description that my 13-year old son had just offered me about the fourth dimension, *"It is soft, like a puppy's ears."* (Said as my son was stroking his puppy's ears!) Yes – Mike agreed. This experience of life felt gentler.

It feels important to say here that Mike already moves pretty fast in his life! I had been teaching him energy tools during our sessions and he was integrating and refining them before he would come back for the next session. He also had picked a partner who moves energy as a pro, seeing patterns and stories clearly, and who is willing to share those reflections with him. So a slow ride through consciousness was not his chosen path!

Within one month, Mike transitioned into the fifth dimension. With ease and grace, and allowing the support of body work integration in his hometown. Now he's viewing his connection to his family, work, health, spirituality... differently! He still works in a very demanding role with about 100 employees reporting to him, but now he's finding that clarity and answers flow easily to help guide his actions.

In our most recent coaching session (two months into the fifth dimension), Mike shared that his greatest pleasure in this journey he's taking through consciousness is the shift in his relationship with his children.

He feels more empowered and sees his role with them now as a solid, grounded guide. He can tune in to what they need from him energetically – AND provide it!

Yes, fifth is fun!

And...

There's More!

Vivienne Gerard

SIXTH DIMENSION

"Delight"

Vivienne Gerard

SIXTH DIMENSION

In the summer of 2016, I recorded a video that I titled *"Feeling the Love."* It was the first of my public reflections about love and consciousness – one week after my transition into the sixth dimension. A few pieces of what I shared then are still the best way to introduce this sixth level of awareness to you now:

'It really doesn't matter what other people say. It matters what I believe. It matters what I know to be true. And what I feel. What I feel in my body.

What I feel right now is so much joy, so much compassion. So much love for my experiences. Forgiveness for the places where I thought I did it wrong. So much love for the people in my life, for the clients I work with, for my family, my friends. There is such an overflow of appreciation and love for this life. And that is really what I most want to share in my videos, my articles, my work.

There are going to be times, obviously, in our journeys where we need to look at some patterns or stories or understand why we do things the way we do them. As we look at those things, we can unravel and clear it. And then our hearts open. Our hearts expand because we realize that nothing we've done is wrong. It's all just been learning and growing.

...Your awareness of life starts to expand. You start to explore what you are here to do.

...When you say to the world 'I've figured it out! It's taken me a while. It's taken a lot of pain, a lot of struggle, a lot of joy, and a lot of adventure, but I've figured it out! This is the thing that I'm bringing forward. And I'm saying to the world – I will die if I don't do this thing or if I don't tell you what I understand to be true.'

And in the claiming and giving of that gift, it's another cracking open of your heart, but in the most beautiful way.

Your heart just goes... ahhhh! I love this world! I love this life! I love my job! I love my family! I love my friends! I love my clients! I love the trees! .... You just have this overwhelming flow of love and it knocks you down.

...As my heart opened again, consciousness expanded again. And I could say, something is different. I understand my role in this life in a different way.

That feels like the Knowing. When you claim your gift and say I'm on my path, and it's THIS direction, you are in this sixth dimension of consciousness. Which really is just this sixth level of opening your heart. It's just more expansion of love. And in that expansion, you have more to give.

SOUND HEALING INTEGRATION:
My Soul Journey
"Feeling the Love"

...You can't NOT talk about it! You can't NOT share it! Because you so badly want people to see – YOU also have a role! You also have something so specific and beautiful and unique to bring to the world.

This love comes from the bottom of your Soul and you want to share it with everyone!"

The sixth dimension feels like a flower blossoming open. In the fifth dimension, you know that there is something unique and beautiful that you bring to the world and you can feel the possibilities of why you're here. You can feel the different pathways that would take you in directions that interest you and align you with your purpose.

ONE DAY

But in the sixth, it is like the flower that has been a bud for a long time finally just opens wide and this flower blossoms. There's a groundedness, a certainty, and a delight.

There is this joy, a bubbling joy that comes from the center of your being that knows that all is well... knows that this experience here as a Soul in a physical human body was your choice. That it was orchestrated to allow you to play! That it was with purpose and intention.

And even if you don't know exactly what that thing is that you're going to be doing in the world, you're clearly on the path of it. You're delighting in the discovery of it!

There is a certainty and a heart expansion that is unlike anything you've felt before.

It feels gentle.

It's definitely a wider, bigger heart expansion with a smoothness to it, a softness. Where the fifth is more abrupt and then exciting, a little scary... the sixth is like a settling, a calming, a sigh. Like you are taking a sweet exhale out into the sixth dimension.

SOUND HEALING INTEGRATION:

GuruGanesha Singh "In the Light of My Soul"

It's this beautiful combination of Spirit really coming down and in from Source, coming down into your physical body. And then the body just expanding sideways out, the heart stretching wider.

Life is a bubbling up of joy in the sixth dimension!

For some people, maybe it's a more intense bubbling. Like for me, I'm already pretty outgoing most of the time. I feel happy and joyous. But, in transitioning to sixth, I couldn't stop smiling! I couldn't stop feeling happy!

I was so excited to talk about how happy I was and how good life is! I wanted everyone to know!

Here, all of your positive attributes get exemplified and you're just MORE! More exuberant! More outgoing! More excited!

If you're typically more introverted or quieter, your sixth dimension will look different than someone who's typically more extroverted. But you're still MORE than you normally are. You still want to talk more about these new ideas, to share, discuss or philosophize, to understand and have that happen through conversation or activity together.

You become more.

It feels like a very physical expansion into the sixth dimension because it's the physical and spiritual locking in together. And as with any transition, this can feel very physical as you shift.

For me, this transition in the summer just knocked me down. Really knocked me down physically, with vomiting and dizziness for a full day and exhaustion that lasted for another day. The physical body was releasing so much emotion, energy, and matter. It was all moving through me... which can feel very intense. While that's not necessarily true for everybody, it is a general statement I would make about fifth to sixth.

STEADYING

And then there is a steadying that happens.

In the fifth, you're exploring who you are and trying to understand more of why you're on this planet and what your Soul wants you to be contributing and bringing from the spiritual into the physical. That expansion might have you feel off balance, a little bit wobbly as you explore. And then in the sixth dimension, there is a landing, a steadying of the experience.

Consciousness expands when it's going to expand... and it's completely different for every individual. There's no predicting it or trying to make it happen.

When you expand from fifth into sixth - your system, your physical body, your mind, your Soul all harmonize. They come into this really beautiful alignment. You feel steadier. You feel more certain. People can push against you and question, wanting you to justify or explain what has shifted in you. And yet it doesn't faze you in the way that it could have in lower dimensions. It doesn't throw you off. It becomes a little easier to be detached or impersonal when those conflicts arise.

As we expand consciousness, it changes us. It changes our understandings of life, our belief systems, and our stories that we have been telling ourselves and that others have been telling us for a long time. Yes, it brings a lot of that up for questioning and then clarifying.

When we feel ourselves shifting and stretching, as I mentioned in the last chapter, it impacts our relationships. And sometimes those relationships can stretch and expand with us... and sometimes others that we've traveled with to a certain point aren't ready to continue traveling with us. They have their own work that they're doing. Their own healing, in their own time frame. And if our time frame is different... theirs isn't wrong and ours right.

SOUND HEALING INTEGRATION:
Bliss
"I'll be waiting"

No-one's time frames are right or wrong – they are simply unique for each person.

Sometimes we can feel that we have to force things to stay the same in our relationships in order to feel safe or comfortable. Or others can make *us* feel like we have to force ourselves to stay the same as we have been.

This phase feels like it offers a detaching from an old belief of, *"I need you to be this certain way in order for us to be happy or okay or friends or spouses or siblings or parent-child, whatever it is. I need you to stay the way you have always been so that we can stay comfortable or familiar."*

When consciousness expands, it's because our Soul is ready for us to create something more or new. To bring something forward that hasn't existed before. As we expand, the consciousness within us becomes bigger, becomes more, and becomes more expressive, which can then create ripples in every relationship around us.

This shift of relationships, when they begin in the earlier dimensions, can feel uncomfortable or even terrifying, like *"What's happening? Am I not going to have any friends? Am I not going to have a relationship with my spouse? What is this shifting all about?"*

As you land solidly in the sixth level of awareness, instead of fear, **you feel a flood of absolute love and compassion for all of the people in your life**... without expecting them to have to be something else.

Just letting them be who they are.

Just letting yourself be who you are.

Knowing it's all perfect and trusting that if a relationship is now complete, it's okay.

SOUND HEALING INTEGRATION:
Imagine Dragons "Trouble"

It's okay if it's complete.

Honor what the journey together has been up until this

point. Find the space of peace between the two of you and allow healing to happen. And if healing can't happen immediately (or ever in the physical), it's okay.

It's okay.

This time of change can feel really overwhelming or intense in some relationships.

Although, *please hear me* when I say that I am not advocating that you leave your husband or your wife, or disown your children, or stop speaking to your parents, or break up with your friends! That is not at all what I'm suggesting. What I am saying is that we are always growing or expanding throughout life and sometimes the relationships that we are in are on different trajectories, different timelines.

If we can each honor and respect what the other person is experiencing and not need them to change or need them to be someone other than who they are in that moment... then the relationships can continue growing. And maybe they continue for the rest of your life and then at some beautiful point, you find each other at the same exact meeting place in consciousness where you're perfectly harmonious.

Or maybe you don't. Maybe the relationship is about each of you pushing each other to be MORE so you stay in close relationship for your whole life, but you're never at the same dimensional level. That can be okay, too. As long as you are respecting and honoring where each other is along the way.

However...

When one person's expectation or will is being forced upon the other person...

When you are being asked or you are asking someone else to be other than who you are...

BROKEN OPEN

By Elizabeth Lesser

"In the more than twenty-five years since she co-founded Omega Institute — now the world's largest center for spiritual retreat and personal growth — Elizabeth Lesser has been an intimate witness to the ways in which people weather change and transition. In a beautifully crafted blend of moving stories, humorous insights, practical guidance, and personal memoir, she offers tools to help us make the choice we all face in times of challenge: will we be broken down and defeated, or broken open and transformed?"

I cried over, laughed through, journaled about, and then shared her stories with those I loved. This book is one of the few in my life that I have deliberately paused reading so that I could savor it longer and not have it end!

"If we can stay awake when our lives are changing, secrets will be revealed to us—secrets about ourselves, about the nature of life, and about the eternal source of happiness and peace that is always available, always renewable, already within us."

Ms. Lesser's story of her divorce gave me permission to come to terms with and then forgive the story of my own. And the wisdom offered through her journeys with many of the world's greatest spiritual leaders are remarkable and memorable. I felt like I was spending hours upon hours with a new best friend… a sure sign that this is a lasting favorite book!

May *Broken Open* also bring you peace and hope in times when you are being challenged.

When someone is telling you how you should be acting, speaking or thinking or informing you what your life's purpose is about and it doesn't match with what you believe to be true for yourself...

Then that relationship needs exploration.

It needs conversation and healing.

When you are putting your will on someone else to change, or perhaps expecting them to advance quickly to whatever higher level of consciousness you are in, then a feeling of superiority or judgment for the other comes in which is not healthy for you or that person.

Their timeline is simply different than your timeline.

The basis for all healthy relationships is mutual honor and respect for each other. Mutual love, compassion, and support for the other one's growth.

When that happens, the relationship is good. It's in harmony.

When one is forcing or trying to control or manipulate the other, the relationship needs to be explored and then changes made in whatever way works best for BOTH of you.

In the sixth dimension, there is a new level of understanding and compassion and certainty that you feel. You know that you are exactly where you are supposed to be. In exactly the teaching relationships you're supposed to be in at that moment.

SOUND HEALING INTEGRATION:
Snatam Kaur "Again and Again"

You honor and adore and love all those who are playing this game of life with you!

All of those Souls who agreed with you to come down

and have this dense human experience. To struggle and suffer through all of the chaos and the fear ... and find their way to expansion and an ever greater Love.

Now you KNOW that life is good.

You KNOW that all is well! Even if it doesn't look so good from the outside yet. There is an inner certainty, an inner acceptance, and deep love for this experience of life.

There's a gentleness that I feel here, too.

In the fifth dimension, there's still a sense of trying, pushing, or using effort that is happening because you're identifying who you are, why you're here, and what you're about. And so it can feel like you're pushing something out into the world. For women who have had babies, the fifth dimension can remind you of your labor experience: *You know you've got to get the baby out but you don't quite know how long it's going to take or what it will be like in the process or if you'll need one doctor or ten or a midwife or what the baby will even look like at the end of the process! So just PUSH!!*

The fifth-dimensional space feels like it holds this pressure to find answers by some sort of self-imposed deadline of when you should have it all solved.

In the sixth dimension, there's just this sense of gentleness, this tenderness.

Your heart expands. You feel more compassion for yourself, more compassion and love for all of those around you.

You're still perhaps exploring what your gifts are or what they look like as you birth them. Or maybe for some of you, it has already happened. You have identified the main work that you're here to do and you're in the process of starting to express that gift to the world.

In the sixth dimension, we begin to claim our brilliance, our gifts. We get clearer on what it is that makes us unique and how we can translate that into something physical here in our world.

Perhaps this is when the idea for a book is birthed, or the idea for a healing center to be started is formed, or this is when you claim your role in a tv show, or your unique version of coaching or teaching, or whatever you are here to do.

The activation happens in the sixth — *"Oh, I've been exploring in the fifth, playing and trying all these things out, and now that I'm in sixth — wwooooahhhhhh, here it is! Here it is!"*

For me, it was the remembering of my Soul's work as a Time Keeper and then how we all begin our human incarnations by choosing one of the five Soul Filters.

MY TRANSITION TO 6TH

Birthing The Soul Filters

My transition to the sixth dimension was in June, the summer of 2016. It was a floodgate of remembering, an opening of all of these ways of being, systems, processes. It was a huge download of information - like the window of my sixth chakra just opened up and I saw so much of what I had forgotten in my human journey.

It was an Activation.

I remembered *for myself* how our origin as Souls before we come into the human bodies offers a choice of what skills we want to work on and what lessons we're here to explore and expand upon for our Souls. And in that choice, we put these filters over our Souls to hide our brilliance and to provide some sort of pattern that we are familiar with to help us bridge the spiritual and physical.

We choose which of these filters we're going to play with and, as we come into the physical form, we're wired and aligned with exploring the lessons of those filters.

This Universal Knowledge took a while to settle into my awareness as I tried to make logical sense of something that seemed so simple yet extraordinary. I had read and studied patterns of behavior and human "wounding" in psychology and energy work, but this Soul perspective was new and SO much more expansive than what I had previously believed to be true.

A few weeks later, I was visiting my friend, Andrea, in Indianapolis and we went to see a friend of hers, Anara WhiteBear, who offers energy readings and sound healings. From the moment she started speaking, I was crying at the purity of the transmission she was sharing with me. I share a few pieces of it now with you because the energy and truth behind the words she gifted me with apply to all of us.

"This time is of great importance. You already know this.

Do this now! Do not hold back. Break through to the next level. You will say yes to the calling you were born for. It was always here. You must honor yourself as a writer — see it in you and claim it. In a new way, recording, transcribing without the paper (which, by the way, is exactly how this book flowed through me!).

When you speak with your words and they keep coming, do not hesitate. There are people around you who would wish for you to be very, very brave and do not hesitate. Who are gathering, continue to gather, who wait for that flowing to come forth. For when you are in the space of the energy moving and coming out your crown and the words are flowing, you are in great beauty.

One being can change an entire experience for many in this world at this time. To say yes to be that being in the reality of many is very brave. And it is Time.

In some ways, it can seem easier to stay asleep and yet to stay quiet. You continue to choose the highest... the biggest. For in doing so, you give to others the experience of the highest and the biggest they can have for themselves.

Any feeling of ego must dissipate into the waters. Being big only means you are free to give the highest parts of yourself. It does not mean you have a big ego. It means you are big like the Sun. Shining brightly so that others may live. So that others may grow.

Be who you already are.

There is nothing which you cannot do."

Anara's words have steadied me over and over when doubt would arise about my work and the path I was following – blindly most of the time! May her clarity bring you the same comfort and steadiness in *your* moments of doubt during expansion.

My friend, Andrea, and I left that session completely drained! We went back to her house to take a nap and then ate and talked for a few hours. Late that night, we were getting ready for bed and chatting about how much we'd enjoyed the day together. She asked me to share the **Soul Filters Story** again with her and decided to record it on her phone as I was talking.

I was feeling playful and happy in this new level of consciousness and started telling it to her as if it was a bedtime story for one of my children. The magic of the moment is still tangible!

SOUND HEALING INTEGRATION:

My Soul Journey "Soul Filters Story"

(I share the text of the Story at the end of this book, but my heart invites you to delight in listening to the audio recording while you read the written words.)

In this time of remembering our Soul Filters, I felt an internal confirmation of *"Oh, okay, YES... I am here to share*

Soul Filters with the world." And when I announced it to my clients and on my website, there was this dimensional level activation. It was the throat saying: *"AHA! Here! This is me, my gift."*

And out rolled this beautiful process of understanding how Souls pick the human incarnation. Through my filter, through my understanding of it.

But that's not always how the transition happens for everyone. For some, your activation may be acknowledging a pattern that has always played in your life and finally looking at it head on. Since it's a significant pattern, you acknowledge it and accept how it's limited you… and then release it, forgiving yourself for all the ways you've judged how you did that thing all your life. This huge internal shift can be the release that transitions you into the sixth dimension of consciousness.

This time is a forgiveness for Self.

An acceptance of ALL that you are, with your perfect things that you do, your flaws, your wisdom, your stupidity… all of it!

You accept that this is who you are and you love yourself.

ONE CONSCIOUSNESS

This time also offers an opening to the collective energy of all consciousness. *What do I mean by that?*

Picture yourself looking out into the sky and then beyond into space, sprinkled with a million, a billion stars… as far as the eye can see on a clear evening.

WIDE OPEN…

Wide open where we are all existing in one energy field. Each of us being one aspect of energy that is connected to the Universe, to the collective consciousness, to One-ness.

Light and Sound and Breath. Expanding.

SOUND HEALING INTEGRATION:
Temper Trap "So Much Sky"

From the very first moment of consciousness until and including this moment in which you read this line in this book... we are all one energy moving and expanding together. Creating new, creating more.

And yet we forget that in our human experiences. We get trapped in the loop of the physical — "P*rove it to me, show me, let me see the tangible evidence of what you are saying in order for me to believe it.*"

So we often feel separate from this Universal energy field in our human lives, disconnected. We think we need to figure it all out by ourselves and struggle through life.

In this sixth dimension, you begin shifting to allow that connection to the one energy field to feel REAL.

Accessible.

Literally sitting right at your crown chakra.

Always.

> Consciousness is an Ever-expanding, Constantly Flowing Source of Energy

That We are All Intimately a Part of In Every Moment.

In fifth, I feel like there are little peeks, sneak peeks where you can sense that *"Woooaaahhhhh, there's a whole bunch of information that I could download into my very empty brain! My very empty consciousness! I could tap in, I could know some things."* But because you're still identifying who you, you don't really tap into the collective in the way that you do in higher dimensions of consciousness.

In the sixth dimension, it's like the top of your crown chakra opens and you have this swirling triangle of energy, this vortex of energy with the point of the vortex at the tip of your crown.

And it's moving, super-fast, very quickly!

It feels like you can reach your hand up through your crown, grab a quick nugget, and pull it down into your mind and then your mind is blown open, right?! *"Woah... woahhhh... this is sitting right above my crown?! I had no idea that all of this information exists or that I had access to all of it."* But it's like little tiny bites, nuggets that come down in the sixth dimension.

Each time there's a nugget of this energetic wisdom, it feels like you have to sit with it for a while and understand it, decipher it, translate it, and then share it in whatever way feels good.

So maybe at first you just share it with a friend and they also say, *"Woahhh... I don't even know what you're saying to me! What do you mean? What?!"* Or maybe it's something you share through an article you write. Or maybe that's when you create a song.

For one of my client-friends, Brendan, he created a comedy sketch with Kristen Bell titled *"Pinksourcing"* about the inequality experienced by women around the world regarding wages. His irreverent look at this sensitive topic resonated through humor! He grabbed a nugget of truth that was timely, pulled it down, poured it into this two-minute video and 15 million people watched, commented or matched the energy of truth that he touched. Powerful stuff!

That pulse... that beat of truth that sits in the vortex above our heads... in the sixth dimension, we trust it enough to allow ourselves to grab little pieces and bring the knowledge down and in.

It is a powerful place to sit. There is a resonance within the Soul, within consciousness, that discerns individually when it is the right time to access it.

SOUND HEALING INTEGRATION:
David Ramirez
"Fire of Time"

Consciousness works in a collaborative way.

It's not something that you can force. You can sit in your meditation and visualize this vortex and imagine pulling and pulling and pulling things down, but it won't have the resonance of truth unless there is an alignment of your consciousness with the collective consciousness.

It can't be forced or manipulated. Access is about setting up this steady practice for yourself of listening, of tuning in, of feeling your own calm and steadiness and readiness for what ALL of consciousness is co-creating together.

And if we're ALL doing that, there is the infinite potential of one beautiful, harmonious action after another... including ALL and expanding ALL.

There is this delightful way that we can play, which we already know as Souls. But now we will be bringing it into the physical.

> Life Literally Becomes Heaven on Earth.

Playing in this sixth-dimensional energy – the spiritual and physical together.

But until we ALL reach that space, what we can do individually in the sixth dimension is create consistent practices of stillness, of tuning in, of healing whatever is coming up inside of you emotionally.

Allowing yourself to feel what is happening in the collective consciousness.

Then trusting that when one of those nuggets comes through... YOUR voice, your activation of sharing it serves everyone.

The more grounded and steady and centered that you are, the more you can hold that nugget of magic that drops in through the vortex.

NAVIGATING THIS SHIFT

In this dimension, you really are working and practicing your vibration, your resonance by setting up a consistent practice of being quiet, of being prepared and ready.

It can feel like an internal time, but for me, it was also such a joyous time! I wanted to talk to everyone! I wanted to tell everybody how amazing life is and how happy I felt! What a shift I could feel in my entire body and how I knew who I was and why I'm here and what I'm here to do.

There was such excitement moving through me that I just wanted to share it with everybody.

And that external activity was balanced with a lot of internal meditation. More sleep. Many quiet afternoons, laying in the sunshine by my pool, just absorbing light. Sucking in as much light as I could. Nourishing my body with minerals through tea infusions. Giving myself good meals, time cuddling and holding and being held and feeling the beauty of the physical form. Walking, running, moving my body.

There is a nurturing of the physical and Soul that needs to happen so that you can be ready to expand more, to hold more.

It is a time of magic!

I believe the sixth dimension is so full of surprises and delights. It is a magical place! I mean, all of the dimensions are, but the sixth... *it is a magical place!*

Now (and always!) is a good time also to deeply connect in with breath. That summer is when I started practicing kundalini yoga, including the Kirtan Kriya, which is a breathing meditation for thirty minutes. I've been doing it nearly every day ever since. This guided meditation offers a powerful way to move energy through your body, through your chakras and clear any stuck places. The chant *"Sa Ta Na Ma"* translates roughly to *"Birth, Life, Death, Rebirth,"* a powerful chant to invite transformation.

SOUND HEALING INTEGRATION:
Nirinjan Kaur
"Kirtan Kriya"

Kundalini yoga, in particular, is a yoga designed to move energy, to bring your body, spirit, heart, mind, Soul all into this beautiful alignment.

It was the practice I chose. I don't even know that I knew I was choosing it for the sixth dimension! But now, with hindsight, I can see that. The yoga practice gave me steadiness. It helped me connect in with my energy in a way I hadn't learned before. It provided a loving yoga community, but still a quiet individual space within that cocoon. My Soul could settle in for some really deep healing and connecting, and my body was in a safe community space so I didn't feel left behind or isolated.

If you don't have one yet, find a practice that works for you to help you align more deeply with your breath.

Because there is MORE coming...

AFTERGLOW

I could not offer a better example of living the sixth dimensional "Delight" than through my client-friend, Brendan, whom I mentioned earlier. A comedian, speaker, writer, creator, actor, and avid reader, he keeps me on my toes when we reflect on life together!

What feels important to share at this time are Brendan's practices that help him expand so beautifully. From the time that we met two years ago, he was already meditating daily and continues to do so still. He is very aware of fluctuations in his energy and has developed many go-to ways to come back into alignment – faster and faster and with fewer big dips. He is on stage often, navigating the energy of a room full of people, and has a practice of grounding before he steps out in front of the crowd.

He is also constantly questioning *"why, how, what does that mean, how do I get clearer, stronger...?"* His internal growth is a priority at the deepest of Soul levels. And naturally, he is expanding so powerfully!

And so when magic comes through the veils, he's already grounded and ready to deliver it and hold the vibration long enough that many, many people can resonate with it.

One other fun nugget about Brendan – he studies people. He reads the autobiographies of people who have the qualities that he wants to embody and then finds the ways to change his thoughts and behaviors accordingly. Not to be like them, but to take the best he sees in life and continuously integrate it into the MORE that he is becoming.

Watch this rising Star... he is what Anara described, *"One being can change an entire experience for many in this world at this time."*

Yes...

...

Let's continue expanding!

Vivienne Gerard

ONE DAY

7

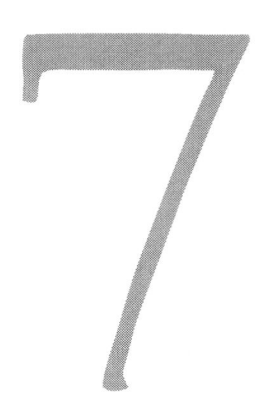

SEVENTH DIMENSION

"Savor"

Vivienne Gerard

SEVENTH DIMENSION

It's funny - as I was getting ready to make this chapter's recording, I wanted a piece of rich, dark chocolate to nibble on. Not to eat quickly, but to take tiny bites of so that I could enjoy the fullness of the treat. Yes, I have the impression that there is a savoring, a sweetness to seventh that is a little beyond words!

Seventh can feel very out of body with its intensity of joy. It really is a time of the crown chakra accessing all of this information and being in the pleasure and the delight of it, the sweetness of life. The deliciousness of it.

This remembering that you are SO MUCH MORE than who you think you are.

MY TRANSITION TO 7TH

My transition to seventh was in September of 2016. My close friend had come over for the afternoon to celebrate her birthday together with an afternoon of talking, playing with energy, and hanging out.

Both of my children had been home sick earlier in the week and so I assumed when I also started to feel sick that morning that it was connected to their flu. Which is what I believe happens to many people as their consciousness shifts – we assume that it's just a stomach bug or dizziness or germs being passed around within the family, classroom or office. It's only later that we can start to piece together the overall pattern and see the connection shifting between the physical and spiritual through our body's processing.

That day, I was sitting with my friend in the living room, feeling queasy, and then suddenly I knew I was going to throw up. After some time in the bathroom, I told my friend that I was sorry but I just needed to go to bed. Not my normal behavior at all to shorten our time!

I laid in bed most of the afternoon. That night, I woke up in the middle of the night and got sick and then passed out on the floor. I remember falling over which must have made a noise and woken my husband up, but we didn't know what happened for a little bit. I felt terrible! I ran a bath and laid still in the water for a while, trying to settle my body before finally going back to bed and sleeping a little longer. And then I felt weak for a couple days afterward as my body adjusted and recalibrated.

It was really an intense transition for me into seventh, but again, I don't believe there's only one way to shift dimensions. Every individual's transition they are going through next is in their own way, with whatever needs to release and move through their body at that time.

For me, from fifth to seventh, there was a lot of physical energy that needed to move out. A lot of old stories, stuff I carried for other people, a lot of energy that needed space to be released and so this transition knocked me down physically. It had me curled up on my side, just listening to music and trying to ground and run energy. And then the transition was over and I was good!

When you're transitioning from fourth to fifth and fifth to sixth, there's a physical but heart-based expansion that is happening. Your heart is stretching and becoming more... you're expanding into more love and more compassion.

What I believe from seventh and on is that your heart is already so full of love, so big that now you're really expanding into the non-physical: your consciousness, your wisdom, your Soul, your knowing. Which is connected to your heart but it's a different sensation, a different expansion than what it feels like up until sixth.

THE MYSTERY OF IT ALL

When you're making the transition into seventh, in particular, it feels important to practice running energy through your body. Working with how energy moves in the physical when it's coming in so quickly, so intensely through the spiritual is a powerful skill.

I believe these energy tools that I share later in this chapter are applicable for any dimensional shift and really for anything you do day-to-day in your life. But for some reason, it feels important to share it here.

So what do I mean by "energy tools"?

First, a little theory:

What I believe to be true is that we are all here as Souls/consciousness in human bodies to experience the physical form in a way that we don't experience as "just" a Soul. And we chose this planet Earth because it offers such a beautiful experience of physical. Even when we judge it and think it's harsh, rough, mean, wrong, difficult or it offers trials or our bodies feel weak here – it is still is a physical experience unlike any other.

Unlike any other planet in the Galaxy.

In the Universe.

Understanding how to move energy through the physical takes practice, awareness, and attention. As we transition between dimensions, we can support ourselves in the process by working with the energy, directing and guiding the energy. So that as the consciousness / dimensional shift is happening, we're aligning with it and flowing with it instead of resisting and trying to control or understand it.

There isn't a logic to dimensional shifts that I have found yet. There isn't a system or process of "you do this, and then it will happen." There is a feeling of mystery and magic that makes it so amazing when you experience it each time.

Consciousness is meant to be mysterious and other-worldly. Wordless.

It is meant to be wordless.

But what we *can* do is support the process by being prepared. By preparing our systems.

By practicing these ways of working and aligning with energy, we can move through the resistance as the shift is happening... faster, with more grace, with more compassion for ourselves, with more understanding from those around us who don't know what the hell is happening to us!

SOUND HEALING INTEGRATION:
Keane
"Somewhere Only We Know"

It's a lot to navigate for the person going through the shift AND also for the people who are supporting that person while they go through it. Transitioning through these dimensions is a lot to understand and support someone through.

So if we have these understandings or awarenesses of how to work with energy, we can use the tools ourselves and also ask our support team to remind us, to coach us through these transitions as they happen.

It's very much like doulas with the birth or death process. The doula offers a steadiness and a different perspective from the outside. They can hold space, coach, encourage and usher that person across the threshold of whatever it is that they are transitioning through.

It is the same for us with dimensional shifts. We can coach ourselves through it, AND we can also inform those around us so that they can co-coach us as we move through it.

For me, the transition to seventh felt rocky or bumpy because I was still in resistance to this process... I didn't understand it. I didn't have a framework for dimensional shifts yet. And the changes were happening so quickly that I couldn't catch my breath or find my bearings physically.

Over the past year, what I have found is that my own journey through these transitions now allows me to better support those around me who are also shifting. I sense or understand what is happening to their physical bodies. Then I coach them by offering these tools that they can use for the spiritual or energetic body to make the whole process a little smoother and gentler.

> **And as One Soul Expands**
>
> **Consciousness *Ripples Out***
>
> **Into Communities.**

What happens is that as one person evolves to the next dimension, there is a ripple in their energy that goes out to those around them and shakes awake their awareness.

Energetically, it literally can look like ripples in the water of a still pond. As the one in the center shifts dimensional levels, it ripples out to the ones around. And then those people start to wake up and shift dimensions. Not everyone, because it's still a unique, individual choice, an individual Soul journey for each person. But the impact of that first pebble dropping in the water and rippling out – that impact is profound as it starts to move through communities, through families and friendships.

And the speed of one can impact the speed of others.

What I believe to be true is that the more people who are starting to wake up and shift through these dimensions of consciousness, the exponentially faster consciousness expands.

SOUND HEALING INTEGRATION:

Chvrches "Clearest Blue"

One shift will impact ten others.

And those ten will each impact ten others.

And so on and so on.

NAVIGATING THIS SHIFT

In this dimensional shift *(which might last a few hours or a few days!)*, it is important to learn the nuances of how to be present to your body and its needs. For me, there was a physical release that my body needed to make of all food, of all hard matter that was in my digestive tract because so much was shifting in my solar plexus *(the third chakra which is connected to the digestive organs)* and its connection to my heart. It felt like a physical purging of what no longer served me energetically.

If you aren't used to paying close attention to your

body, now is the time to start! When your body is signaling to you that you need to throw up, you need to release, my suggestion is to acknowledge and honor that and just flow with it.

Be tender with your body. Set the intention as your body is releasing that you are aligning with gently letting go of whatever it is energetically and physically that your body is trying to send OUT and away from your space. Don't judge yourself or try to stop the releasing process. Let it literally just move through and out.

So, my first suggestion would be to align with your body and trust it. Trust that your body knows exactly what is most needed.

And then rest. If possible, clear your schedule for a day or two if you have things that you are supposed to be doing. Let yourself lie in bed and simply be still.

Drink water.

Trust what your body is telling you that it needs. Whatever the craving is for the food or drink that you are wanting to put into your body, trust that and give your body that gift.

It may be that you need more minerals and nutrients to help ground your body. If so, make some tea infusions. You can look up how to do that - it's super easy. Better yet, have tea infusions prepared all the time so you have them available! And then when you have a dimensional shift, a bottle of magic is right there in your fridge ready for you to fill your body up with healing.

Definitely sleep during this time more than you normally would. Let your physical system acclimate to what's happening. You are literally changing the cells in your body. Energetically, spiritually, you are shifting your cells to a different vibration. And so it's not something that you force your way through, or push your body to manage.

THE TRUE POWER OF WATER

By Dr. Masaru Emoto

Dr. Emoto's introduction says it all...

"Dear Reader, I am honored that you have picked up this book. In a world of no mistakes, it is not by coincidence that you and I are embarking on this journey. The words and pictures you are about to see will open a new world of possibilities for you — just as my research has done for me.

In this book, you will learn of the unique properties of water and its ability to improve your health and your life. You will see the effect each of us has on water — not only the water we drink but also the water that makes up 70% of the human body and, most importantly, what happens to that water as we interact with each other.

... It is our individual responsibility to learn all we can about water, the most precious resource on our planet, and to help shift the consciousness through our thoughts, through our words and prayers, and through our commitment to respect each other with love and gratitude. May our understanding of water help bring peace to all humankind."

Why should every person on our planet read this book? *"We must pay respect to water, and feel love and gratitude, and receive vibrations with a positive attitude. Then, water changes, you change, and I change. Because both you and I are water."* Once you see images of water crystals before and after changing the language around the water... you will forever view our most precious resource differently. Thank you, Dr. Emoto.

You gently honor whatever the body is experiencing and allow it space to heal and become new.

Become new.

Become more than it has ever been before.

Did I already say Drink Water?!

Drink a LOT of water.

Bless the water.

This time really is an incredible dance of physical and spiritual. It takes space, kindness, gentleness, and compassion for Self to allow an easy transition to unfold.

ENERGY TOOLS

The other thing that I would suggest in this transition and beyond is to visualize how energy flows through your body. If you already do this, these next suggestions might add to what you currently practice. And if this is all new information, the key is to simply play with your imagination!

Energy is the magical spark of creativity, which means that the only real limits are the ones you and your mind put around your imagination.

Energy play – one of my absolute favorite things!!

So consciousness shifts to me, at this level of seventh and above, look like downloads of light coming in through the crown chakra. Those can be controlled to a certain point… if you are putting your attention on them.

What do I mean by this?

Well, when your body starts to signal that something

feels different - but you don't quite understand what is happening - but you know something is shifting and it's not your average virus or stomach bug - you just know something feels more intense or different in this moment... simply start to visualize the energy.

1. ENTERING YOUR CROWN CHAKRA:

Close your eyes, sit quietly, and imagine you can see your crown chakra, the space at the top of your head about an inch or two above your physical hair. The space that receives this invisible connection all the time to God or Source energy.

Some people visualize that connection as a cord, like a bungee cord. Some people visualize it as light, liquid, or sparkly gold dust. There are a million ways that you can visualize your connection to Source. For me, I like to visualize it as a light beam that comes in, a bright white light.

As you feel yourself shifting physically, as you feel something becoming different in your body and you believe you may be having a transition to another level of consciousness, you simply turn your attention to your crown chakra. And "look" or "see."

What does that connection look like in the moment?

If it feels like there's SO much light (love, wisdom, information) trying to come through a tiny, tiny little hole at the top of your crown chakra, imagine you can open that crown opening a little wider. Dilate it, so that if it is only a tiny little pin drop of energy that is able to currently come through, imagine you can widen the opening to now make it the size of a quarter, or the size of the palm of your hand. Perhaps you want to make it as wide as your head.

You'll know. You'll feel what is comfortable.

And then you can visualize as that opening expands that the light is flowing easily down and in through your head and running down through your body.

If it feels like there's too much downloading and you want LESS coming in because it's too intense or fast or overwhelming... imagine there's a little faucet with a valve on the side, right above your head and you can simply lower the volume or flow. For example, if it felt like 100 miles/hour of energy flowing into your body, turn the pressure down to 10 miles/hour or 1 mile/hour.

You can work with the energy to come in at a pace that feels more in alignment with where you are in the moment.

And that might change in the moment!

You might feel how AMAZING this huge flood of light is that is coming into your body! And then just five quick minutes later or an hour later, you might be groaning *"Woahhhh... I can't manage all of this!"*

Okay, so slow the pace down or turn the faucet volume down or make the hole/opening smaller to "manage" the energy flow.

You're not going to lose the new information, the connection, the expansion of consciousness. You won't lose it by slowing it down. You'll just make the transition gentler on your body.

YOU set the pace when you focus and put your attention on it and when you bring your awareness to your crown chakra. You set the pace.

2. MOVING THROUGH YOUR BODY:

And then you can feel that light as it comes into your body. You can track where it is going with all of your cells.

You can track it moving through your head or you can

have it massage your shoulders. If you've been carrying the weight of the world as you moved through your fourth, fifth, sixth dimension and now you have this next shift and you're coming into seventh... you can just exhale.

You can allow the light to come down and through your shoulders, massage them, and soothe them, as if the light is saying *"Oh, you think it's been YOU all this time, that's doing all these things in Life?! No, no, my Love. It is and always has been a co-creation between Source AND you! And I am right here with you, pouring light and love into your physical body."*

Now you can allow Source energy to be your partner, your ally, your co-player in this game, instead of you believing you did and still do it all by yourself.

SOUND HEALING INTEGRATION:

Coldplay "Yellow"

You can bring the energy down and through your body, running it down your arms, running it through the inside of your body, soothing every single organ as the light comes in and changes the cellular structure of your body.

You can imagine it as a white, healing light so that it's re-charging each organ with each touch. The light is healing the places that in the physical body have perhaps felt depleted or worn or damaged.

This shift to the seventh dimension is again a *consciousness* shift. It is a shift in the connection to your spiritual and energetic source of Life... of ALL.

If there are places in you that need healing, align with this beautiful energy that is arriving. Invite your physical body to receive the spiritual power that moves through.

How?

By relaxing each organ, each muscle, each bone.

Which then allows more space inside of your body for healing to occur, for rejuvenation to happen.

> **We are just at the Edge**
>
> **As a Society**
>
> **Of all the Healing that is Possible**
>
> **Through Light**
>
> **Through Source**
>
> **Through Intention.**

We are just at the beginning of it.

In this shift of consciousness, let your body feel the perfection of how you were created.

The perfection of the potential of who you are, as a Soul- human- physical- spiritual- energetic combination.

And then run the energy.

Visualize this light, sparkle, or whatever form you have the energy in as it moves through you... visualize it moving all the way through and down to your feet. And then use the pace and depth of your breathing to settle your body and allow it to expand at a cellular level.

Allow your cells to get bigger, fuller, more vibrant, and more alive.

Breathe into every cell in your body.

Breathe again.

Breathe...

3. GROUNDING INTO THE EARTH:

And then feel the connection of energy gathering at the bottoms of your feet. Keeping your life force energy inside of your body, visualize the extra energy forming into roots that grow from your feet down into the dirt underneath your body. Then visualize those roots spreading deep and wide into the Earth... all the way to the center of the Earth.

Notice how your entire system gets steady...

Gets quieter and calmer...

Breathe...

...

Running energy – it's that simple! And beautiful.

This process is one that you can do every single day to continuously align yourself with your expanding consciousness.

These are also tools that you can use in the moment of a dimensional shift. In the moment of consciousness transitioning where you feel like your body, perhaps every part of you is exploding or falling apart or feeling completely disconnected.

SOUND HEALING INTEGRATION:

Christina Aguilera "The Voice Within"

By bringing your awareness to the way the energy is moving through you, by visualizing the light at the top of your head and then managing the flow of it, visualizing it moving through your body and down to your feet and into the earth...

You become the conduit of the energy.

So you're not resisting the energy. Instead, you're aligning with it and allowing your body to be a riverbed that it can flow through. And the energy just keeps streaming in and through.

The magic is that as you're doing it in this dimensional shift, the energy is literally changing your cells as it comes in and moves through your body and goes into the Earth.

What it looks like energetically to me is a string of brilliant lights, sparkling, like a million white holiday lights, sparkling inside your body! Like confetti that is always moving!

It is an incredible process to run energy in this way. Perhaps simply align with it, gently feel it, trust it and surrender to it. Instead of resisting it, you can completely change your experience and it will be so beautiful.

So beautiful!

ONE CONSCIOUSNESS

The seventh dimension offers a clearer connection to Source energy.

In the fifth dimension, you are starting to know your gifts and open up more to your incarnation experience, bringing Source energy down and into the body, trusting whatever it was that your Soul wanted to create and do in this lifetime. Sixth is when you really start to activate what those gifts are and you allow more clarity about how you're going to deliver your Soul's purpose.

And then in seventh you are really accessing the collective energy! Really feeling the oneness, the speed of connection, the speed of consciousness, the speed with which information can flow. Knowledge can come from above and down and in so certainly, with such confidence.

The seventh dimension is expansive.

It feels like the veil between worlds lifts... the window opens more and you can see your place WITHIN the collective energy. You can feel how your gift starts to ripple out to honor and support all of those other Souls who are here on this planet with us.

SOUND HEALING INTEGRATION:

Coldplay "Speed of Sound"

It's sweet. It's tender.

It is very much about connection. But not in a way of *"I connect with you and so you owe me something, or we have to have this thing we both do."* It is a connection as in *"I see you in your brilliance. I honor where you are. I honor who you are."* And there really isn't an attachment to it of *"something has to come back to me"* in that place.

Seventh still feels very grounded.

Very inspired. Delightful and light, lively, joyous. There is more light in your physical body in seventh.

There is more breathing room. The breaths are deeper and bigger in the seventh dimension.

ADVANCED SOULS

One thing that I haven't discussed yet is that this book is written assuming that most people are in the third dimension when they are born and make their way into the higher levels of consciousness throughout their path.

There have always been Souls *(but especially at this time)* on this planet who incarnated in higher dimensional levels than third in order to fulfill their life purpose. As they came in, their consciousness already was at a level above the density of fear in the third dimension. They chose that as a way to hold space for humanity to evolve. To remind Soul-humans of the potential that exists for each one of us to create more.

As the number of Souls incarnating on Earth continues to increase, the density of humanity has gotten exponentially heavier and more difficult to step out of or to evolve through. In response, there has been a balancing need for more Souls to come in at the higher levels of consciousness to hold space for humanity's evolution, to show the way to expanding consciousness, to support more evolution of these higher dimensions.

For those Souls coming in at these higher levels of consciousness, they will only expand. They won't become less than they were before in this human incarnation. They won't go backwards down the level of understanding, of being, or of awareness.

AND they also have their own Soul's path of what they are here to learn or experience. Maybe, for example, they come in at a fifth or sixth level of consciousness, but they still feel the density of fear, judgment, criticism, and lack. Even with their advanced level of Soul evolution, they still work through those same human energies that those in the third dimension of consciousness are working through.

Every Soul-human is always clearing and releasing and advancing their consciousness.

It just comes at different places. We do our human work at whatever level of consciousness we are experiencing.

I believe many creative artists come in at seventh- or

eighth-dimensional levels of awareness and they use their artistic gifts to inspire and resonate with humanity through music or image or the beauty of creation. They use their gifts to wake up the desire for MORE in the density of the third dimension.

Prince is a perfect example of this creative magic sliding through the density of humanity. His song, *Purple Rain*, is known word for word by millions of fans and was honored with such reverence by fellow musicians after his death. If you listen to the lyrics, he offered such a powerful sound healing of forgiveness, love, and compassion. The energy and healing of his gift rippled out around the world for years, touching so many hearts.

One of my favorite songs by an artist that is timeless is *Imagine* by John Lennon. When I described in the sixth dimension how we can reach up through the veils and touch a truth that is Universal... I believe that is the gift his song brought to humanity at a time when we desperately needed to believe in dreams and unity.

SOUND HEALING INTEGRATION:

John Lennon "Imagine"

Even if you have heard this song a thousand times before, I invite you to pause, find the song, close your eyes, and take five minutes to hear the lyrics from this new way you are exploring of Love and consciousness. You will be inspired.

There are countless other visionaries and leaders who have held this pure, clear belief of One-ness for all of us. What a gift to still feel their Love in the physical expressions they shared and continue to share with us.

AFTERGLOW

As I have been writing this book, the parallels and synchronicities have been arriving one after another! It felt like a portal opened when I started the first audio recording four months ago and Source energy has been playing with me ever since in new and fun ways.

This next Afterglow is a perfect example.

I started working with my client-friend, Erin, last summer, right as I was transitioning into the sixth dimension. In our first session, I already knew that she was firmly functioning in the fifth dimension, with the most beautiful, wide-open heart. She had a few layers of story and old patterning to clear, which we moved through very quickly. Did I mention she was getting married three months after we started our work together?! Arriving at a threshold as powerful as that is often a catalyst for a significant expansion of consciousness.

The weekend of her wedding was Erin's transition to the sixth dimension. Her heart cracked open and love literally radiated out to everyone within her and her new husband's sphere. You only have to hear a few of the moments she shared about her wedding day later to understand the impact a pure vibration of Love can have as it ripples out into communities.

For the next five months, Erin kept working through blocks in different areas of her life, exploring patterns that she wanted to shift… expressing her voice in clearer ways.

Then a few weeks ago, we hopped on a coaching call and she started describing these "strange" symptoms that she had been experiencing for a couple days… which were very similar to what I shared earlier in this chapter. I positively muscle-tested my theory that she was transitioning to seventh. When I shared it with her, she agreed with all of my descriptions.

Part of what was initiating her shift was the potential decision with her husband to buy their first home, which had brought up a lot of emotion and fear to be explored. In our prior session, we had cleared a few of her blocks and visualized the joy of the two of them having their first home, walking through the rooms, growing a garden in the back yard... a fun exercise!

That session was on a Wednesday. That Friday, Erin and her husband found a house in exactly the neighborhood they wanted to live in... with ALL of the items on their wish list. The current market in their city, though, is a true buyer's bidding war that significantly increases the purchase cost for every home. No fear needed in the seventh dimension – they had their realtor immediately contact the seller and make a direct offer. One day later they signed the paperwork for their first home with their original offer accepted, no counter-offering or bidding process necessary. *So fun, right?!*

The beauty of this story is that it doesn't end! When consciousness expands, it becomes more. And more.

Erin and I spoke this past week and her first words (after we celebrated her new home!) were *"Things are just different. Easier. Coming more naturally."* Yes, that's how it feels. She's finding internal motivation to take better care of her body and to cook better meals. She's creating spreadsheets for her husband with the details of their plan for their new home (this is usually his gig!), not because he asked but because she can see how clearly things can be streamlined and communicated.

Things are just simpler. And most importantly – she's so happy! Happier than she was even when I first met her right before her wedding to the man of her dreams.

Yes, it just keeps getting better.

... Oh, wait – there's More?!

EIGHTH DIMENSION

"Bliss"

Vivienne Gerard

EIGHTH DIMENSION

From this moment on, my invitation is to begin integrating sound into our journey together more deeply. If you have not yet played a suggested sound integration, no worries... AND please begin now. The music, the lyrics, the energy of each song adds depth and range to your experience of my written words.

It is much like eating a delicious piece of your favorite food. If you gobble it up in one or two bites, it is over too quickly and just leaves you feeling unsatisfied and wanting more immediately. If you take your time and savor each bite, feeling the fullest beauty of the moment as it unfolds *(enjoying where you are sitting, who you are with, how your body is feeling, what your eyes are seeing...)*, then the moment is embedded within your heart and your memory for always. You will not feel unsatisfied.

You feel complete and satiated.

The remainder of our journey together can unfold with deep intimacy and true connection from one Soul to another Soul... and sound is that bridge of depth.

Take your time, read, pause, find the song on your phone or computer, close your eyes to listen to it... to FEEL it... and then come back to the written words when you are ready.

This book is waiting to walk with you, alongside you as you expand. So please fully savor this experience of allowing Bliss through the eighth dimension of consciousness.

Vivienne Gerard

**PAUSE...

What I share next might bring up questions if you have not explored these ideas before, but my belief is that our fears are often just of the unknown. Once we allow awareness and explore ideas new to us, we find that the unknown is not scary – it is exciting and full of possibilities that our limited minds might not have been willing to open up to before.

What if everything that I share next is true? What would that mean to you? What could possibly shift for you? How could this new information expand your Love?

SOUND HEALING INTEGRATION:

The Moody Blues "Question"

Be curious and see what opens in your Soul.

We begin this chapter by bridging two different ways of being in this world.

The first way is the path that many of us have followed to this point and the one that I've been describing throughout this book: evolving through one level of consciousness in the physical plane to the next until we arrive here in the eighth dimension. LOTS of struggle and density, misunderstandings, contraction, expansion... and now finally, arriving at this place of Bliss.

Where we now know and trust that Love is eternal and flows constantly through us.

I will call this path – a Gaia Soul Tribe Expansion.

The other way of being is where we BEGIN by knowing and trusting that Love is eternal and flows constantly through us and our Soul embodies this Universal Love. From birth throughout our childhood and tender teenage years all the way into adulthood, we see and feel Love in everything. And yet no-one else around us is getting it! And the struggle is that we can't seem to help them understand it, no matter HOW MUCH we love them.

We wonder at times how we even landed here on this planet filled with density and so much fear?!

Welcome, Star Beings.

In this chapter, I am writing from BOTH perspectives, to allow a space for healing any separation so that from here on... we all expand as one.

WELCOME, STAR BEINGS

The eighth dimension is where a lot of Star Beings have come into this planet.

What do I mean by a Star Being?

Eighth-dimensional Star Beings are also Souls like all of those playing here in the Gaia Tribe. They are beautiful channels of Light and Love *AND* they come from all of the planets in the Universe. Their "home" planet is not Earth, but they visit here as Souls from time to time.

> **SOUND HEALING INTEGRATION:**
> The Lumineers
> *"Stubborn Love"*

These Souls play a different role than the Time Keepers described earlier because they move *between* the planets, which allows them to see and communicate among all forms of consciousness existing in our Universe. Whereas the Time Keepers are mostly focused on their own planets *(yes, each planet has its own Soul group of Time Keepers)*, until, like now, where we are all doing this collective work to assist one planet (Gaia) through a pivotal energetic shift. And hopefully one day, for one moment, at one point in another dimension, our Gaia Time Keepers will also be able to support the Time Keepers of the other planets and ... more magic!

But in this moment, it feels like many, many eighth-dimensional Star Beings are here on Earth to share wisdom and hold space for us as we heal this planet. So their messages are very optimistic. Very focused on love and healing and bringing everyone together.

Soothing the places where people have fear.

Holding this really clear vision of what is possible for humanity. Providing road maps for groups and individuals of how to find our way forward. Really beautiful magic!

For the adult Soul-humans who are functioning at that level on the planet now at this time, and for the children who have been arriving at that level over the past ten to fifteen years, they are complete channels of Source and collective Unity.

Powerful and beautiful examples of Pure Love.

That is what the eighth-dimensional Star Beings bring to us – Pure Light, Pure Love. The ones who are grounded and feel secure in their environments and safe, trusting in the human experience, are bringing us the most incredible wisdom and messages.

Such magic, such hope, such optimism. They can see how everything always connects and some of them are translating it so beautifully for Soul-humans as we struggle through the density and confusion.

And yet, they are also here to have human incarnations, which means they experience the range of emotions of humanity – fear, pain, disappointment, judgment, and on and on! They are here to expand their own consciousness through contrast, and their challenge is bridging how clearly they can SEE the potential for Love and then BE that Love in the physical form.

Living in this divide of knowing the Truth and yet not having anyone around you understand it in the same way is deeply painful and can feel isolating at a human level.

And so I share the next two sound integrations to offer compassion and then inspiration for all Star Beings who might have a match… and those in relationship with and around them. Allow yourself to touch the human despair… that then leads to greater Soul strength and clarity… and then the reminder, the certainty that Source Love is ALWAYS present, ALWAYS guiding us forward in this physical – spiritual – physical – spiritual exploration.

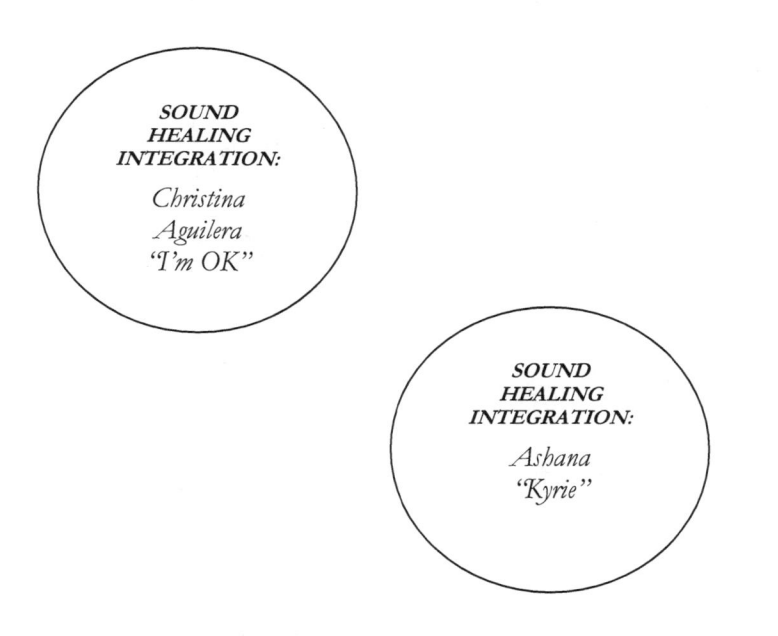

SOUND HEALING INTEGRATION:

Christina Aguilera "I'm OK"

SOUND HEALING INTEGRATION:

Ashana "Kyrie"

JOURNEY OF SOULS

By Dr. Michael Newton

One of the best books to read if you are especially feeling the confusion or pain of isolation or of not being seen or understood for your gentle spirit or open heart is *Journey of Souls*.

"Now considered a classic in the field, this remarkable book was the first to fully explore the mystery of life between lives. It presents the first-hand accounts of twenty-nine people placed in a 'superconscious' state of awareness using Dr. Newton's groundbreaking techniques. This unique approach allows Dr. Newton to reach his subjects' hidden memories of life in the spirit world after physical death.

While in deep hypnosis, the subjects movingly describe what happened to them between lives. They reveal graphic details about what the spirit world is really like, where we go and what we do as Souls, and why we come back in certain bodies."

I read this book when I was going through my divorce, seeking answers to the questions that my mind couldn't solve logically. The stories shared by these Soul-humans offered my heart a new level of forgiveness and understanding in ways that no counselor or friend could during this time in my life. Since then, I have witnessed the veil between this physical world and the spirit world that Dr. Newton spent his career describing becoming thinner and now dissolving into clearer and clearer visibility.

May this beautiful exploration of the afterlife open up new possibilities in your consciousness.

I find that here especially, sound is a powerful and gentle form of communication and Love connection that transcends differences in Soul stories, cultures, languages, histories, or beliefs.

As I mentioned in the last chapter about advanced Souls, many gifted musicians and artists are bringing us the same Universal message:

> **They are Reminding Us**
> **That We are All**
> **One Collective Consciousness.**

The more we can each believe this truth, feel it and allow in support through music, meditation, and community – all of these beautiful tools that we have... As we allow ourselves this support, we will be able to align with the flow of the Universe in easier ways and stay in that flow and trust.

What Star Beings already know and are sharing with us is that the eighth dimension in its purest form is just BLISS!

Bliss!

And joy!

And certainty.

So expansive. There are no edges to where the eighth dimension goes out. To me it feels like this horizontal, infinite, stretching out... of space, of love, of energy, of connection. This horizontal rolling wave of sound and light.

SOUND HEALING INTEGRATION:
Snatam Kaur
"Heart of the Universe"

It's stunning!

Eighth dimension is stunning!

AND it's simultaneously interesting in the contrast it presents to humanity of spiritual/energetic vs. physical.

I can see why it is challenging for many eighth dimensional Star Beings to function in a third dimensional reality of 9-5 jobs and money and deadlines and clothes and food and housing... all of that feels so limited and stupid! It takes time and effort to hold onto all of those things, maintain all those things, fix all those things, prepare all those things – it can feel endless and pointless.

Instead of staying where the energy field is so perfect and beautiful!

Why and how do you choose day after day to go into the limitations of the third dimension and function in that "reality" when the eighth dimension feels so beautiful and pure?

It feels important as a Guide to pause and offer a reflection here on the contrast that can feel so intense to a Soul-human at this level. I share more about this again in the next dimension, but it's relevant really at any stage of consciousness.

It is a choice.

Every day in every moment.

The human incarnation on Earth is a physical experience with emotions and "wounds" and stories that can feel so real in the moment we are living them or as we hold onto them from our past.

When we are expanded at this level of consciousness, feeling open and vulnerable...and then people we trust hurt us or "wound" us...

The pain can make us want to shut down or disconnect from the world around us.

What my heart offers as Truth is that the "wounds" are all illusion.

It's all part of the contrast of the physical. When this human journey ends and our bodies stop functioning while our consciousness moves back into the non-physical form, the Earthly "wounds" are revealed for the stories our Souls always knew they were.

And we realize that we just got caught in the density again. *Silly us!*

Remember that *"exciting, beautiful, powerful loop – Soul to human, human to Soul, Soul to human, human to Soul…"* that I described *alllllllll* the way back in the third dimension? We can feel caught in that loop at any point throughout our human journey.

And so awareness of the loop is always the first step to changing any painful story.

All right – so let's go back to the question on the previous page about *why and how we choose to stay engaged in a third dimensional reality when we know all about the beauty of the eighth dimension?*

My answer would be that we are here to expand Love and consciousness and always be creating more!

And it is most needed in the third dimensional reality of this Gaia / Earth.

Yes, we forget that at times in this journey through the dimensions of consciousness.

I believe that is why more and more communities are forming and growing, like in Sedona and Boulder. Star Beings are gathering their Tribes of other eighth-dimensional (and above) beings and are now feeling seen and witnessed for their gifts instead of shunned or ridiculed for being "different" or not understood.

As these Tribes gather in the physical and develop deeper connections, there's also a rising collective energy that happens... a synergy.... when everyone brings their attention to one place and harnesses all of that knowing together. Then there is so much more room for magic to happen! The channels and downloads from Source through these Guides are that much clearer and consistently validated. And then we're just off and running into this great wide open playground of Universal joy and expansion!

It is a beautiful thing to see these pockets of wise and loving Souls gathering. May more and more form and feel safe and valued in sharing their gifts with our world.

NAVIGATING THIS SPACE

What does the eighth dimension feel like in your body as a Star Being?

It feels like your energy is bigger than your physical body. You're definitely out of the body chakras. It can be different for everyone, but as I tap in, it feels like I'm energetically outside of my head, above my crown chakra. My energy feels like it has a forward momentum, like wanting to go into the future. Or a sense of hovering or hanging above my crown, like I want to energetically go out into the sky.

There's definitely a natural state of wanting to be OUT of the body, above the body, connected to light, connected to sound, connected to love. The body feels heavy and limited.

So the beauty of a Star Being - Soul who is trusting eighth-dimensional energy is when they are IN their body, coming all the way down and in... and they ground.

They connect their energy through and into the Earth.
Why?

When you tap into that Earth energy and you connect deep down like the root of a tree, then all of that knowing from the eighth dimension... all of that certainty and trust and love and unity can flow down and through and just emanate out of you through the Earth and into the communities in which you function.

Your clear, grounded energy can flow out through technology, across the internet, and connect and gather Tribes virtually.

SOUND HEALING INTEGRATION:
Anugama "Chakra Journey"

But the secret, the key to it is the grounding.

The feeling of anchoring in your energy — through your feet into the Earth. This process can feel a little intense for Soul-humans who have been functioning in the eighth dimension for a long time and channel all of this beautiful Universal information.

Grounding down into your feet can feel very restrictive and "roped in," which doesn't feel good to everyone who is in this level of consciousness or above.

But at this time on our planet, that is what is most needed...

To anchor into our Earth.

To allow all of that energy that is available from the Collective, Universal Consciousness to come down and through the body. Then whatever YOU aren't needing, whatever your body isn't using, you just channel into the Earth which then powers up the energetic grid of the Earth. Yes, YOU help power up the energy center of Mama Gaia that is healing right now.

So this process of grounding makes you a human lightening rod as you provide a protective connection that transmutes the high vibrational energy from Source down into the ground of the Earth.

You are a Conduit Of Energy.

That energy from Source – that light wanting to pour into this Earth – can find your energy connection, your grounded center point, and literally, help power up the center of the Earth. Crystallize – wake up the crystals in the core of our Earth.

As I write this, I can feel my own Soul calling to people who resonate with this concept of eighth-dimensional energy to start grounding yourself to the Earth. To root yourself into the Earth energetically and allow those downloads to come through.

Please don't hold tightly onto the currents that flow in, just allow them to move through you into the Earth. What you need to feel or charge up for your physical and spiritual self can happen... and the extra just goes into the Earth.

There's no loss to anyone.

It's just a different way to work with the energy that serves so many more humans, so much more of consciousness when you can run it through you into the Earth.

Exhale...

...

THE GAIA SOUL TRIBE EXPANSION

And now the other way of being! For those of us who are following a path of ascending to eighth, who have been moving through all of these previous layers and are now coming into the eighth dimension, welcome to Bliss! This dimension feels very similar to seventh, but wider and without end.

In this space, it feels like you are taking up more room – your energy is expanding and there is no limit to where you can expand to here as a Soul-human. There's no limit to how you can connect through time and dimensions and energy fields, with anyone, and with any memory.

SOUND HEALING INTEGRATION:

Liquid Bloom "Whispers of Our Ancestors"

It feels like your energy is literally expanding outside of your physical body space. Which can be a little disorienting for some, especially if you've been moving through the dimensions quickly. If your Soul is on this accelerated path to go through the dimensional levels quickly, when you go from seventh to eighth it can be very disorienting to have that much energy space tangibly feel available to you.

What to do?

The same thing I would say to someone who has been in eighth for a while – stay in your body. Ground energy all the way through your feet and anchor yourself like a tree root into the ground. And then just allow yourself time, rest, and nourishment so that you can integrate what is happening in the physical body and gently accommodate, adjust to this new feeling of your physical body being aligned with eighth-dimensional energy!

It's a lot to adjust to, especially if it's been within a short amount of time!

YOUR SOUL'S PLAN

By Robert Schwartz

This is the only dimension where I offer two suggested book readings, as we make a pivotal shift from physical "reality" to spiritual KNOWING.

"So often, when something 'bad' happens, it may appear to be meaningless suffering. But what if your most difficult experiences are actually rich with hidden purpose – purpose that you yourself planned before you were born? Could it be that you chose your life's circumstances, relationships, and events?

Within (this book) are stories of ten individuals who – like you – planned before birth to experience great challenges. Working with four gifted mediums and channels, author Robert Schwartz discovers what they chose – and why."

Oh are you in for a beautiful journey with this book! There is something so powerful in following the actual life story of an individual, seeing the ways that their choices determine their next experiences. Unravelling that all the way back to when he/she was a Soul making those options a part of his/her Soul Plan … wow! I found each case study fascinating.

For all humans and especially those who struggle with addiction, grief, depression, anger, feeling victimized or limited – these stories offer a different viewpoint that may open your heart to shifts that are possible in your understanding of your own life's story. Such peace and acceptance…

ONE DAY

The eighth dimension is so beautiful.

If you haven't been experiencing it yet in your human journey, this is definitely where your dream time space can become magical. You can have conversations with anyone in your dream space and it's just beautiful. And you will remember the dreams – they begin to feel as real as your waking life in some cases.

I started journaling my dreams when they were particularly memorable and even now when I go back through my journal and see just one or two lines, I can give you a full, detailed, clear account of exactly what was happening, what the space itself looked like, the sequence of what unfolded. The dreams often provided guidance or cleared emotions that were apparently needing my attention energetically.

It's a powerful process to simply witness as an observer from the sidelines.

This time is tender as you step into a field of energy that is Universal. It's remarkable.

It feels quieter in the eighth dimension.

It feels more peaceful to me. This is the place where music can literally bring you to tears. Watching children, watching nature can just humble you.

SOUND HEALING INTEGRATION:

Donna DeLory
"Blessed Always"

You can feel Presence in the most incredible way.

As we bridge the gap between Souls who are from other planets and Souls who have incarnated to Earth over and over, Presence is the place for us to meet and heal. Simply being present in each moment, we can surrender our judgments and expectations. We can feel how similar we all actually are, wanting to be seen and validated and valued.

One of the greatest shifts and gifts happening on our planet right now is an expansion of the definitions of Love and Presence as seen through our children.

I believe the eighth dimension is where we can find many of our "labeled" children with ADD/ADHD, Asperger's, Autism – children who are identified as being "on the spectrum." My understanding is that many of these children came in as eighth dimensional energies / Souls into physical bodies. Part of their "work" is to teach all of us how to be more present and also to help us feel the magic of what they inherently know to be true:

That there is this collective energy that they represent and it is beautiful.

It's Love.

It's Life.

It's Kindness.

May we learn these deeper lessons from them and open our hearts (and consciousness) ever wider.

AFTERGLOW

As we evolve into these higher and higher levels of consciousness, the word "ethereal" often comes to my mind. Ethereal – *"extremely delicate and light in a way that seems too perfect for this world."*

Yes, that can feel true when we meet Soul-humans who are this connected to Universal Consciousness. It seems like they can look right through you into your Soul!

My client-friend, Heather, fits this description perfectly. She is stunningly beautiful and also appears delicate, even fragile. Inside, though, is a solid and fiercely-centered Soul who knows she is here with a big purpose to fulfill in this lifetime!

Do not be deceived by appearances... these are wise, powerful Souls who understand the intricacies of humanity and still choose to come have these Soul-human journeys.

They have SO much to share with us.

Heather is an Artist.

A highly creative and talented designer who has successfully navigated the fashion industry for her whole career. Like all of us, she has worked through the density and emotional struggles of being human. But she has a passion to create MORE... to bring more beauty to our physical world through her art. She understands the power of inspiring others through fabrics and textiles that please the senses, delight the eyes, and melt the heart.

And so, as a grounded eighth-dimensional Soul-human, she is getting better and better at running energy into the Earth and allowing the downloads from Source to simply flow in and through.

As she does so, her capacity to hold more and spread her foundation wider keeps increasing.

Her vision – *"I am bringing together a global collective of artisans and small businesses. As Creative Director of my brand, I am selling my designs and products, as well as curated products from other makers that fit my aesthetic or are slightly adjusted to fit my aesthetic."*

Here is a peek at what Heather stands for in her work on our planet:

"Ethical manufacturing is essential to the health of our brand as well as our planet. We raise awareness through our responsibly made products, using ecological practices that reduce pollution and waste, as well as support communities worldwide. As the consumer becomes more aware of how her food, skin care, and lifestyle affect her wellbeing

and the planet, she expects her clothing and accessories to follow suit. We use organic and recycled textiles where available, and support artisanal small businesses."

These are the leaders of consciousness who are changing how we exchange within communities and through our supply channels – with deep respect and love.

And we continue expanding into More…

› ONE DAY

NINTH DIMENSION

"Precise"

Vivienne Gerard

NINTH DIMENSION

The ninth dimension also feels out of body. It feels completely spiritual, energetic. A very high energy, but also an ethereal level of consciousness.

Clear.

Very specific.

I noticed as I was recording the audio for this dimension that I spoke noticeably slower, taking the time to make specific word choices because the power of the word is so clear.

The power of sound and light is also so clear in the ninth dimension. Many musicians and elite artists are creating in ninth dimensional energy. They understand the power of lyrics, music, sound notes. The power of light. Light from within and external light, reflected light, radiated light.

Sunlight.

Spotlight.

Ninth dimension feels tingly, vibrantly alive. It feels like you want to jump out of your skin! For me in this moment of tapping in, it feels high-adrenaline. Like my energy is way too big for my physical body – it doesn't fit.

The access to the energy or download feels so fast. I imagine songwriters and poets here can literally just sit down and write the words perfectly without a need for edits. The artist in ninth dimension just sits down and creates the art.

There isn't a struggle or effort to the creative process.

It's simply this flow of energy that is tapped into the Universal current of energy. The limitation is in how fast the physical body can channel or download what is coming through and allow it to be captured in a physical form, here in a physical, third-dimensional world.

The pace feels *sooooooooooooooo* slow and dense in the physical world which is why I believe some ninth-dimensional Soul-humans turn to narcotics as a way to help the physical move as fast as their energy is moving. But it's too intense for the physical to align with narcotics long-term – the physical body can't keep up.

It can't keep up.

The secret for ninth dimension, the guide of how to integrate it is actually *the opposite*. Perhaps now it has been feeling like you need to move faster. That the adrenaline needs to rush and push and move through you and let you go, go, go.

The *opposite* is actually what integrates ninth dimension.

So Stillness.

A meditation practice.

A beautiful example of this high-vibrational energy being harnessed and integrated into the physical can be seen in the iconic Tina Turner. If you read about her life story, she has shared publically that her practice of chanting allows her to flow the energy from spiritual, from consciousness, from universal love… through her physical body in a focused way.

> **SOUND HEALING INTEGRATION:**
> *Crown of Eternity*
> *"Ra Ma Da Sa"*

And look at the powerful and beautiful ways that her body moves and shares energy with millions of people!

Take a little time to read about her Soul-human journey and allow it to perhaps inform your own.

Once again, I suggest exploring Kundalini yoga as a way to gather all of your high-vibrational energy and then in stillness, through chanting, specifically target how that energy moves through you into creative output.

This is why Kundalini yoga is so powerful. It has the ability to show you how to align with the highest vibration possible while being solidly in the physical body. I am a firm advocate that exploring the alignment of a Kundalini yoga practice is worth the time for anyone moving through ninth dimension and higher.

If not Kundalini yoga, what else would serve?

Any mindfulness practice that has you integrate your energy and then blend with the physical in a quiet, reflective space.

Swimming meditation is coming to mind because the water is quiet and meditative and your energy is so focused in your body.

Chanting, for sure. It's sound, energy moving through the mouth, vibration, channeling, and using intentional words.

Rowing is coming to mind. Yes… you're in the water and there's a rhythm to it. Rowing with intention, with focus feels right.

Rowing, swimming – there seems to be a theme of water showing up, also!

Ecstatic dance!

Ecstatic dance combines high vibrational energy with physical movement in a way that allows for individual expression. So, yes, ecstatic dance.

What else?

Om-ing. Om-ing through orgasm allows the energy and the physical to align with pleasure.

Cooking. But cooking with intention and deliberate creation, feeling the intention of the foods. You flow with the energy that moves through the foods.

Really, art of any form.

IF the art is just moving through you without judgment. When you bring judgment in, you start to impact the flow in a negative way, which then blocks the creativity. The judgment blocks the flow and then you're resisting, you're struggling against the ease of the ninth dimension which makes the physical feel difficult… which can make you want to check out.

This dimension is very much about surrendering to and trusting the Divine energy within each of us.

The Source energy within. Really trusting and knowing that pure love, pure energy is guiding your actions.

Ninth is VERY intuitive. It's not the old masculine-based doing.

The only action is coming from inspired action, which is coming from the feminine-based, intuitive knowing.

So there's no need for effort or pushing in the ninth dimensional vibration.

It is fast speed-wise, fast flow-wise, but intentional.

And still.

And precise.

Focused.

The energy is felt more intensely in the fifth chakra and above, the upper chakras. As I tap in right now, I don't feel the lower half of my body at all, the energy is all up high.

THE REASON I JUMP

By Naoki and KA Higashida

"Written by Naoki, a very smart, very self-aware, and very charming thirteen-year-old boy with autism, this one-of-a-kind book demonstrates how an autistic mind thinks, feels, perceives and responds in ways few of us can imagine. Parents and family members who never thought they could get inside the head of their autistic loved one at last have a way to break through to the curious, subtle, and complex life within. ... With disarming honesty and a generous heart, Naoki shares his unique point of view on not only autism but life itself. His insights are so startling, so strange, and so powerful that you will never look at the world in the same way again."

Last October, I sat down with a large sheet of paper and downloaded phrases of high-vibrational words from A-Z. Not sure what to do with this information, but knowing it was somehow a gift to share with children who were on the autism spectrum, I went to the bookstore and scanned through the books on autism. Many from parents, doctors, and specialists... and then this magical book straight from a Soul-human who is teaching US about life and love. I went home and read the book straight through, my heart opening wider and loving Naoki's courage and commitment to communicate with the world, despite so many obstacles.

This is a book to share with your children, grandchildren, students, and then every adult willing to receive powerful wisdom from a child.

Blessings upon blessings to you, Naoki.

I believe that is why when they're in the physical form, for many ninth dimensional Souls, the body feels too intense. Unless they can create this physical-spiritual combination practice daily or every other day to come back to the flow of Source, to the flow of the energy, the ease of the process, and the ease of the dimension.

When you feel disconnected from that Divine flow of energy, then the physical limitations can be too stressful and too frustrating. The conversations in the third-dimensional "reality" around you are too dense, too heavy, too depressing. There's a feeling of *"nobody gets me, nobody understands this. Everyone else is out of alignment, I'm in alignment. How can I be in this world when there's no-one else in alignment with me? With Source? With Love?"*

This feeling of disconnection and isolation can become paralyzing for many Soul-humans at this level of consciousness.

These are the times when I turn to music.

As I was typing this section into the manuscript, the song *"Bleeding Out"* played on my music shuffle. I include it on the next page as a suggested Sound Healing Integration to say that I see you, the one who is feeling misunderstood and alone. I get it. I have felt that isolation, that sense of separation from the rest of the world that seems to have life all figured out in a way that makes no sense to me.

And also, a gentle reminder – our Soul knows that it is all simply an illusion. We don't have to *"bleed out."* Not for ourselves and not for anyone else.

We are all here to expand Love and Consciousness and learn from each other. None of us individually have the answers or solutions to make this human incarnation an easy ride at all moments. Every one of us hits tough roadblocks at times, places where we are struggling and don't know which way is up or down.

> It is Simply Our Belief
> That We are Separate and Isolated
> That Keeps Us
> Separate and Isolated.

How do I know?

Because I remember at my core that I chose this human experience. Source didn't force me to take on physical form to come suffer and be alone. Why would Source do that?

Source is Love.

Always.

If you don't trust my words, please consider trusting the music, which I know was being guided by Source as I write this for you today.

The next song that played on my shuffle was *"Sweet September"* which (of course!) opens with the chant of *"Ong Namo"* – the exact words and sounds that opened this book.

Followed next by *"Long Time Sun."*

I invite you to pause now and find these songs on YouTube.

Close your eyes and truly listen to the lyrics and the melodies as they speak to your Soul.

Explore the contrast in the experiences of each song and connect them to your Soul-human Journey.

Feel the Truth that sits inside of you.

> **SOUND HEALING INTEGRATION:**
> Imagine Dragons "Bleeding Out"

> **SOUND HEALING INTEGRATION:**
> Alicia Mathewson "Sweet September"

> **SOUND HEALING INTEGRATION:**
> Snatam Kaur "Long Time Sun"

Source energy is sitting right here with you, INSIDE you... in the exact moment you are listening. We are never separate from our Source energy. It is just the density of the physical experience that can create the feeling of separation.

So what do you do in these moments?

Tune back into your way of connecting to Divine energy.

Create your daily practice that combines the physical and the spiritual and allow the flow of Source energy to become easier and more consistent.

Start finding your Tribe.

Trust the ways you are being guided to be in community and allow yourself to build new Soul friendships here on Earth. If you don't know where to begin, come join the Soul Shine Tribe virtually through Facebook. I am holding the space and it is a gentle and loving community of wise Souls.

This is such an important time on our planet for ALL Souls to keep expanding – yes, even beyond the ninth dimension!

As we all keep evolving, our gifts become clearer and stronger and we can step more and more firmly into our unique ways of guiding and helping humanity to heal.

The more Souls who are grounded and connected and practicing their mindfulness (realigning every day to this ever-expanding energy), the more voices we have who are doing this, then the less isolated Souls in ninth dimensional consciousness and above will be on our planet.

And when these Souls find our Tribes, hearing other voices who are connecting at that same dimensional level of consciousness, we will feel clearly seen and deeply validated. We will recognize others with the same vibration. And then as a collective energy, we can begin expanding into the next level of consciousness.

This is already happening in our world.

The more people who are hearing, seeing, and accepting this message of Love and Consciousness in the fourth and fifth dimension, then the more Soul-humans who are expanding and evolving into the next dimension beyond that. As more and more people are shifting, Love is rippling out in larger and larger ways.

> SOUND HEALING INTEGRATION:
> *Caspian "Separation"*

So as someone sitting in the seventh, eighth, or ninth dimension is hearing more familiar voices and feeling more vibrations and sounds that are like his or hers, then they will settle into that vibration more...

Expand...

Expand...

And then *whoooooooshhhh*....

Pop into the next dimension!

Like an accordion file, consciousness will just keep expanding wider and wider and wider.

Without end...

(I am offering two Afterglows in this dimension, to show the ways that consciousness moves us forward, whether we are following the "traditional" path from third dimension onward or arriving in the human body as a Star Being energy.)

AFTERGLOW

In the sixth dimension, I described a healing session that I experienced with Anara WhiteBear. In the nine months since she guided me through that powerful shift, I have witnessed this beautiful Soul-human continuously land more deeply in her own gifts, sharing them in wider ways.

Anara is a Star Being. A beautiful clear channel of Pure Love. When you first meet her, you see the exterior human shell - a gorgeous woman with big blonde hair, biker-hippie clothes, a huge hug to greet you, and these piercing blue eyes that look right into your Soul. And then she opens her mouth to channel wisdom during a sound healing and Pure... Love... Pours... Forth...

Her human journey has not been an easy or simple one. Yet, she would likely tell you today that she has finally found her Tribe. First in her Love partner, Chris, who sits solidly by her side and provides the grounding elements of deeper sound to support her ethereal sound during a session. And then in the community she has joined in Arizona and around the world as she begins sharing her healing gifts more openly and clearly.

Here is a tiny sample of the wisdom Anara shares in her weekly transmissions *(from March 25th, shared with permission)*:

"IT IS TIME NOW for you to release your fears for what is coming. Fears. It is that which you have feared.

You have chosen to step forward. You have chosen to create something very different than what has been created before. And you have done so in a time when all illusion has been relieved and revealed. For in the illusion there is tension. For in the illusion there is tension, listen to these words. This is spiritual stress when you are living in illusion. When you are trying to be something that you feel others want you to be. This is illusion.

For in saying, I will go forward you have also said, "I will no longer live in illusion. And I will do my best to be open every day. To see differently." And so, as these energies build, and you have been given the opportunity to see through everything, it is not only your personal depths you are going to, you are going to the collective depths because you said yes. I will go and I will see. I will experience something different. ...

So now you watch the collective begin to wake up and they are not waking the way you woke. Their waking is shocking to them for their illusion was safety. Their illusion was safe to them although you always saw, you always knew, this is not real.

And so, in these days that come, when the illusion is shocking to the collective, you hold in your heart the love you always have for them. Yet, still, there is an uncovering for you as well. For though you thought you could see clearly, there are parts of yourself, the illusion, that is allowed to be viewed now. To say the levels that you are going to are difficult is not true. They are what you asked for, they are real. And they are actually simplifying your being.

As the collective lets go, so do you. ... You are taking steps now to experience something you have never experienced before. And this has to do with the loosening of the collective. For in that way of being that the collective has held, it has held you from experiencing more. ... And so you begin to get used to the multidimensional way of experiencing reality. To feel as if your expanded consciousness will not stop expanding in the moment. And that you have no control over what you are experiencing.

This is the next level of letting go. Without any help of hallucinogenics, without any help of anything that adds to your experience of more. When you are quiet, when there is nothing in your system, not wine, not tobacco, not mushrooms, not even ice cream, that which brings others joy, without having to ask for help, the help is offered for the expansion of your consciousness. You understand that it's happening now, your consciousness has reached levels that now is, is, IS creating a new reality.

There is no turning back from the change in the way that your brain works. There is also no need to explain, for even those who you thought did not understand are now beginning to see that there is more. The less you speak, the less you try to explain, the more they will understand and they will ask you questions. ...

We say to you, BE who you are, be the Star Beings. ...

Do you understand that this makes you a Master? Do you understand that you are here because you are already a Master who can embody all at the same time in the physicality, in the physical, in what you know as the 3D? You are a Master. We are not in the physical as you are. We embody another frequency, and we embrace what you have chosen, we embrace this in honor and respect."

I end this nugget of Anara's journey, quoting the words she uses at the end of every Facebook post...

"There is only Love."

AFTERGLOW

Oh, how my heart melts just in the knowing of the Soul-human I am introducing you to in this Afterglow. My friend, Andrea, was the activator at the beginning of my awakening, taking me to see my first psychic and guiding me through the loss of my dear friend / her Soul Love in our late twenties with reading suggestions and clarity about Love being infinite.

We both agree that we have walked this human journey many times together before, playing all types of roles with and for each other! We are each other's guides and space holders in this lifetime, celebrating every expansion.

So, Andrea's journey through consciousness...

Earlier in this chapter, I describe how the belief that we are separate or isolated is what actually keeps us separate or isolated. It's not actually our truth, it's an illusion that helps us learn whatever lesson it is that our Soul wanted to explore here on Earth. But it feels REALLY REAL in the human living of it! This applies to her story.

Andrea is a Moon-Orion Soul Filter, who thrives on taking care of those she loves and being in a community. Her Tribe for much of her earlier life was her immediate family and she was deeply needed in that group of Soul-humans. As she had her own daughter, her Tribe expanded to include those in her daughter's community. And then the family of her partner who died. And then more. And more. And more!

She juggled loving so many people very well, but the weight of supporting others emotionally and physically through being a care-taker took its toll on her own physical body. On her emotions. She lived in the stress and confusion of the third dimension's fear and limitation (like so many of us!) for much of her life.

Until early 2016 when she started experiencing the bouncing back and forth of the fourth dimension. Seeing the shifts happening in her life… but coming back into the limitation and beliefs she'd held for so long. Back up into the possibilities and joy… back down into the density. So frustrating, right?!

And then last summer, she had a huge breakthrough and landed solidly in fifth. She remembered the power and beauty of her Soul – the one who had lived so many lifetimes before, guiding herself and others through this Soul-human dance.

In the "reality" of remembering these lives, she cried at the lifetimes where she had been abandoned or isolated. Where she had been the healer and drained her own energy to take care of her community. She felt the lessons that those lifetimes had taught her and started putting pieces together, weaving a pattern that showed her how much

ONE DAY

wisdom she actually had to draw on from within herself. She realized that SHE was the one in the center of her own experiences here in this lifetime. SHE was creating her community – it was being formed by her choices in every moment. And no, she *wasn't* actually responsible for *everyone* around her.

This is a HUGE shift in consciousness that ripples out throughout every relationship when it happens. We begin empowering everyone around us when we claim our OWN power first.

So for the past nine months, Andrea has been putting herself in the center more. Asking for support as much as offering it. Receiving AND giving. Becoming more visible in her own gifts. *(She blesses homes and helps people claim and then consciously create the energy of their living spaces – SO awesome!)* Using her voice more from clarity and knowing.

And she has rapidly moved from the fifth through to the ninth dimension *(as I write this today)*. Some of the transitions have been physically tough, knocking her down for a few days as her body lets go of more old stories and beliefs. Emotions have come through in waves, strengthening her trust in herself more and more. It's absolutely incredible to witness!

Here are a few reflections from my beautiful friend:

"The shift from one dimension to another – I believe that every Soul experiences it. Even if they're dabbling back and forth from third to fourth and they never actually land in the fourth. There are shifts happening in all of us all of the time! Shifts that we're not able to identify or give a name to or reason. Which can be confusing and overwhelming.

So we're still learning how to recognize it.

The more I experience and move through energetic changes and blockages and growth… it just makes sense that we then elevate ourselves to getting to a place of more and more compassion and love and understanding and non-judgment. Which is ultimately where we reside more fully in our gift and our life purpose.

Do not let hiccups come in and divert you from your Truth. Bump it all up to the next level.

I'm here to tell you, keep bumping it up!

Enjoy the beauty of your labor as you birth your gifts.

It's all okay.

Sometimes experiences can make us question everything that just this morning or yesterday afternoon or five minutes ago felt so beautiful and in perfect alignment. We know how good that feels. And then the contrast — something shows up where we feel the doubt or self-consciousness.

You know how to move through this.

Be gentle with yourself. Be tender. Continue to call upon all of the support in your Tribe.

All is well."

10

TENTH DIMENSION

"Steady"

Vivienne Gerard

TENTH DIMENSION

Until 2012, the tenth dimension was as far as consciousness had expanded in the Universe. Then there was this shift in 2012 where consciousness (Love) began expanding into more. And we went out to the eleventh and then to the twelfth dimension that year and stayed at that edge until 2015 when we bumped out to the thirteenth dimension... and now even more and more.

It is so fast now.

The expansion is so quick.

By the end of 2017 *(the year I am writing this book)*, I don't know what dimensional level we will reach. My guess is the seventeenth dimension. We are at fifteen right now and it is unknown what is being co-created next or how it continues expanding.

We have never been at this level of consciousness before now. It's all new.

It is all new.

So, let's look at the time leading up to 2012. For a long time, if we are using Earth measurements of time, we have had this consciousness awareness of what I will call the tenth dimension. And that was the infinite space, without limits, for so long. There was just this ever-expanding field of energy that went sideways, up, out.

SOUND HEALING INTEGRATION:
My Soul Journey
"Nothing Becomes Everything"

It was quiet.

It was what perhaps some have called the Void.

The Nothingness. When you reach this dimensional level, you dissolve into nothing and become part of everything.

The Void is full of potential.

It actually holds ALL.

For millions of years in Earth time, the NOW moment that we know in consciousness expanded out infinitely but the dimensional number we would have assigned to this would have been ten.

In the ancient Mayan calendar, the reason that 2012 was so important is that we reached a tipping point in consciousness where more light entered our planet, more energy was being created by the power of technology, electrically being created, AND we had magnified focus and attention from so much of humanity on this one moment of time. This all combined into a powerful moment of expansion that popped us through to the next level of consciousness, which was eleven and then, almost immediately afterwards, twelve.

But those are recent dimensional levels that have been opened up. This is the true beginning of the co-creation. Everyone bringing their attention to expansion and pushing us through to the next evolution, to the next understanding.

In the tenth dimension now, today, what it feels like in 2017...

It feels very steady.

Very calm.

The tenth dimension is a very consistent connection to Love and God and Source and all other humans. There isn't a desperate seeking anymore for answers or understanding.

There's just this quiet knowing that all is well.

All is well.

And we are expanding more and more and more.

There is an acceptance of people for who they are, without needing to change them.

> SOUND HEALING INTEGRATION:
> Deuter "Temple of Silence"

There is an acceptance of all of the "blocks" – the word that we would have used in previous dimensions – blocks, resistance that life presents to us. We see that those are actually just stories, energies, teaching lessons for us.

We settle into this rhythm in the tenth dimension of…

Calm.

Grace.

Love.

We're still human, so we still have life come up to test us and teach us. We still have a range of emotions that move through us… but the emotions move faster. The "blocks" are noticed and transmuted fairly easily.

And we return again and again to Love.

THE GENE KEYS

By Richard Rudd

"This book is an invitation to begin a new journey in your life. Regardless of outer circumstances, every person has something beautiful hidden inside them. The sole purpose of the Gene Keys is to bring forth that beauty – to ignite the eternal spark of genius that sets you apart from everyone else. The Gene Keys are a complete set of teachings designed for modern life. Through the ancient art of gentle contemplation, and through reading and applying the wisdom of the Gene Keys, you can discover the higher purpose of your life."

Every word in this description is true. I started reading this powerful book in January of 2016 and it took me a year to contemplate and begin absorbing the wisdom of all 64 Gene Keys. Mr. Rudd weaves art, science, religion, history, and spirituality in the most incredible way. I would read a chapter while eating lunch at home and then ponder the mystery of it all for days.

The beauty of this book's journey for me is that the Gene Key I would be reading about at that time always EXACTLY mirrored what was going on in my life! I would find the guidance I needed to release another layer of story or resistance and move deeper into my journey of consciousness with even more love than before for myself and those around me.

Please gift yourself with the time and space necessary to walk through these Gene Keys in deep contemplation. You will be amazed at what you discover and who you become along the way.

YOUR SPIRITUAL PRACTICE

Your spiritual practice, whatever it happens to be, is what keeps the tenth dimension feeling steady as a Soul-human. By the time you evolve to this level, your practice is so firmly established that when you aren't in that daily routine, you feel immediately that you're out of alignment.

There is a physical craving for the spiritual peace that you feel in that quiet, reflective space.

That settled, peaceful feeling inside of your body becomes your baseline of how you want to show up in the world.

What I have found in the tenth dimensional space is that resistance simply presents itself to test your commitment to your walk: *How secure are you in your practice? How important is it to you? Can you consistently prioritize that routine for yourself?*

For me, I could feel the resistance testing my commitment through this constant push-pull on my time.

If I only have so many hours in a day and a set number are dedicated to taking care of my family and pets, serving my clients, managing my home and business, eating, sleeping... where is the time I need and crave for meditation?

For journaling?

For walking reflectively in nature, delighting in our beautiful planet?

For laying in the sunshine and soaking up light?!

For simply BEING?

This is the perfect time for a reminder that YOU are the one in the driver's seat of your life.

I know, how many times do we hear that and groan or roll our eyes? But feel the truth of those words.

YOU determine where your time is spent each day, even if you feel that you are limited or restricted to what others are telling you to do.

You can make changes at any time, and your path will shift to reflect those changes.

And then you adjust and explore what you want to create next... and the path shifts again.

> SOUND HEALING INTEGRATION:
>
> *Alicia Mathewson* "Breathe In Breathe Out"

And so on and so on.

I was the one who had to say that my meditation time was now going to be scheduled into my daily activities and that it would happen every day.

EVERY day.

Non-negotiable.

I found that when I meditated in the morning, the first thing to do on my "work schedule," the practice quickly turned into a comfortable routine. Then I played with increasing the amount of time I would spend meditating, adding in guided meditations and ending with quiet stillness.

Now I include chants and mudras in that daily meditation time, which I love for the movement and focus of body and mind simultaneously.

AND... my practice now happens every day, even if the time of day moves around because life is constantly changing!

What I find over and over is that this daily meditation practice helps me focus on how to most efficiently use my "limited" physical time each day and identify easily what my priorities are – from my Soul.

When the guidance is clear and specific, it is so easy to get a LOT of stuff done in a very short amount of time! In Gay Hendricks' *The Big Leap*, he calls this "Einstein Time" – the ability to bend time when you are flowing in your creative mode of genius. Very true!

It feels important to add here that this testing of commitment in the tenth dimension simply feels like a strengthening for our Souls. It doesn't feel like a judging, a criticism, or a place where we are less than or not measuring up to some unknown standard.

The testing feels like it strengthens my resolve.

It strengthens my commitment to stay steady.

To flow love through me.

To do my Soul work *(whatever that is for each of us)*.

To do my Soul work with clarity, love, compassion, and certainty.

The tenth dimension offers a **Knowing** that the Soul work each of us is here to do is vital for the co-creation of our planet.

> **You are on the Leading Edge of the Shift That is Happening in Consciousness on Our Planet.**

You have reached the former boundaries, edges, or limitations of consciousness. You have moved into this space now where it's quieter because there are fewer energies in this space… but it is more focused, more deliberate, more intentional.

And each Soul has a unique gift(s) that they agreed to bring and share in this co-creative space. To guide our planet through these shifts of consciousness.

In the tenth dimension, there is a certainty and a momentum, a forward motion that carries us, that can't be resisted.

It feels irresistible.

Through this momentum, we access greater levels of universal knowledge.

For me, one of my gifts is guiding others in meditation.

So in the tenth dimension, I can access how Source would guide a meditation in the highest potential for all of the people on the call in that NOW moment. I can feel and sense what that flow of love is and allow that energy to move through me and out to the group gathered.

For some, if your gift is cooking, this is the space where you align with the universal knowledge of food *(what most serves the human body, how best to prepare it, what foods heal illnesses...)* and allow that information to guide how you're doing your cooking. And then share what you learn with others!

If you're a writer, you align with the flowing of wisdom that will most serve our planet. And share it!

An artist, a musician... you are in alignment with the highest potential of what Source energy would bring through to our consciousness of planet Earth at this time. And then please, please share your art and music with us.

SOUND HEALING INTEGRATION:

Fleetwood Mac "Songbird"

In the tenth dimension, there is this easy flow of high

vibrational energy that is constantly coming through the crown chakra, wanting to be expressed.

Love... Light... Gifts to be shared.

This Soul-human journey really is about joy and love and pleasure.

Play.

In the tenth dimension, you are very conscious of your physical body and it's alignment with spiritual energy. There's a reverence for the physical body. This is why we want to honor what we feed our body and the experiences we create for our body. We want to give it more rest.

We fall in love with our bodies in the tenth dimension if we haven't yet. And we understand the true gift of this human incarnation, every time we experience it.

Gratitude and appreciation are the powerful emotions that flood us and allow the expansion to always continue.

AFTERGLOW

A few years ago, I met this gentle, joyous Soul named Andrea through a women's leadership group that gathered virtually each week. We got to know each other over the phone first and I fell in love with her sweet spirit, constantly being amazed at her deep wealth of knowledge about the body and how it heals. We met in person at a retreat at my house two years ago and from then on... lifelong Soul Friends!

Andrea is a gifted acupuncturist and healer, who was creating self-care products to support her clients and friends as a side business. That passion is building into a beautiful empire called **Andrea's Alchemy** – healing products that help our bodies integrated the energetic and spiritual changes happening here on Earth.

Each client that I work with energetically needs physical support to anchor in the shifts they are moving through, and Andrea intuitively knows what most serves their bodies. It is an amazing healing combination!

As an Advanced Soul, she has lived most of this incarnation sensing things about those around her that perhaps they are not always ready to hear. Offering her wisdom but not having it valued for its powerful gift. Often, this can make one start to put up walls or shut down the flow of information. Andrea simply channeled it into her education and studies in Eastern Medicine. In her early thirties now, she is wise WAY beyond her years!

When I first started to understand dimensions in this clear way, I was sharing with Andrea a few reflections and asked her if I could check in on her dimensional level. When she said yes and I started muscle testing, I immediately got ninth dimension and was so surprised! I knew she was wise – but WOW! Super cool and super advanced! We played with how she was bringing that Universal Knowledge here into this physical world and have had many conversations since about this dance of consciousness.

Since then, Andrea has been "doing her work," as I like to say when those I love are really moving through their junk, releasing old stories and patterns!

And... she has gracefully shifted into the tenth dimension. Landed in this new place of quiet, joyful and full acceptance of her life.

Knowing that she is the co-creator of all that is showing up... and precisely, deliberately focusing her power on what she chooses next.

Here are a few of her reflections about her shift:

"Everything is really just good!

I feel like I keep saying yes to the things I want to do instead of listening to the fear that used to stop me. Now I really just love my life – I love the way I live my life!

I feel more confident in everything I'm doing. Whereas before I worried about what other people thought a lot more – like about how much I wanted to travel and where I spent my money or my time.

But, this is what I want to do - I love to travel. So much! And now I don't care what other people think! And I'm allowing in support in my relationships which lets me go travel. Which is awesome!

I don't know that I've ever felt this way – ever. It's pretty exciting! I've been in gratitude more and focusing on what I have versus what's missing. One of the reasons I used to get so frustrated is that people around me couldn't get it and I would think, "Ohhh – it's just right there in front of you, it's so easy to see!"

It's almost like a weird new patience now. Definitely different.

I feel happier than I've ever felt before in my life and it's awesome! I've always had highs and lows but this feels so consistent. One of the things I've been claiming is that Mondays are no different than a weekend. I want to be excited to get up every day!

I've also been having this thought lately that I want to make money while I sleep! So, I'm exploring ways to do that with my work and through investing and I'm listening to financial podcasts that are inspiring me. I'm excited about that – even if it's just a little bit of money each month! It's smart for me since I'm self-employed.

All of these desires have helped me have better boundaries. Now I'm not focused on how many clients I do or don't have because it's all just energy flow anyway.

Everything feels much easier in my life. I'm super grateful! And it's good because a lot of people I know are struggling right now and it feels good to be a support to them, offering what feels like really solid advice.

A huge part of what makes me feel better is choosing to do the things that make me happy, like walking in the sun and getting exercise. I just want to keep learning the things that can make me better.

It's really not about other people at all, but about always being better yourself!"

Ahhh…. Her joy is tangible! Embodied. Grounded. Infinite. Yes, it is possible to be all of these qualities at the same time.

And there is still more…

ONE DAY

11-12

ELEVENTH & TWELFTH DIMENSIONS

"Realm of Dreams"

Vivienne Gerard

ELEVENTH AND TWELFTH DIMENSIONS

The eleventh dimension evolved in September of 2012.

I believe this evolution is what Esther Hicks describes in her audios as *"The Vortex."* When we all *"send rockets of desire into The Vortex,"* we expand the energy field because so many rockets of desire are all being pushed against the limitations of consciousness. And this pushes us past what we knew before.

When more and more people are stepping into their gifts and waking up and expanding into these higher levels of consciousness, all of that expansion pushes against old limitations... stretches out... and MORE gets created.

And as more gets created, consciousness expands beyond what it was before.

It's the same process that began with the Original Breath.

When Source was one Original Breath and breathed more, six Elders were formed from this Original one Breath.

SOUND HEALING INTEGRATION:

Crown of Eternity
"Ang Sang Wahe Guru"

And when each of those six Elders breathed more into existence, we stretched beyond what we were before that.

As more Souls are birthed or breathed into existence...

And more Souls incarnate in human bodies...

And this population of physical humans with energetic Souls continues to expand on our planet...

...we are all co-creating more and more.

Which pushes us ever further at a faster and faster rate in Earth time, in human terms.

If you only look back over the past one hundred years of life on our planet, for example, it is incredible how much has changed in our daily lives. Especially in the last twenty years with the expansion, *explosion* really, of technology.

Every new idea sparks other new ideas... and our world is literally changing right in front of our eyes, daily.

As I said in the last chapter, in September of 2012, we moved from the tenth dimension and popped out into eleven and then twelve very rapidly after that.

What that simply means is that the energy fields expanded.

The attention of many, many Soul-humans in spiritual-physical form became focused on this one time-date that had been anchored in place by what we consider to be wise teachers from so long ago. The attention that was put many, many years ago by the Mayans on December 2012 had always been bringing focus to this time as a significant moment. Add it all together and this laser-focused concentration of energy fields suddenly popped open these new dimensions of consciousness starting that September and all the way through December. *(Which might have felt like the end of the world to some people!)*

We rocketed open new levels of consciousness, new understandings of consciousness.

It happened because our attention was on Time... a specific, fixed moment of time.

And so we broke a pre-conceived limitation about time. We shattered a long-held illusion of the Mayans supposedly predicting that time would be finite. That we would hit an end date and things would *"collapse."* Perhaps we misinterpreted and the meaning was actually that things would *"expand."*

I believe that this energetic shift started with the Y2K fear in 2000 that technology couldn't keep up with time changing at the changing of the century-mark, but technology was also mixed in there with time so it wasn't quite as clear a focus.

2012 was actually just "Time."

Putting our focused attention on time, having an ending, and then realizing it didn't end and that time is literally just a series of NOW moments… we expanded consciousness, we expanded awareness.

Our Elders walked us through the portal.

Of course.

And more light flowed into our planet.

More love flowed through.

As this shift happened in 2012, being in the eleventh dimension felt like you were out in the Universe stepping into the sunrise.

Like the image I offer on the back cover of this book – when you see the sun coming up over the horizon of planet Earth from outer space, there's mostly darkness with that one line of light shining right across the middle of the horizon. If you can imagine being there in space, standing on the top of the planet… feel yourself moving through the darkness toward that new horizon of light. Absolutely incredible!

SOUND HEALING INTEGRATION:

Caspian "Rioseco"

The eleventh dimension felt a little ahead, a little out of reach as it was unfolding.

It felt like you were literally out on the edge of the Universe... guided by the Light... guided by Source... knowing the way is forward but being absolutely in the dark... blinded in how to get there... clueless on how to navigate in this completely unknown level of consciousness.

There were a few Souls in 2012 who started to play in that space immediately. Mostly Elders and some Time Keepers from other planets. It feels like it was an exploratory space of consciousness for a little while (in human terms). September to December 2012 was a period of a lot of energy moving and expansion happening very rapidly, as shown by the quick movement out yet again – into the twelfth dimension.

As an Elder pushes through the previously known edges of consciousness and guides us into a more expanded consciousness, it's like a release valve for all of the levels that had been expanding within those original boundaries. All of the energies pushing against the back of those limitations can then move forward and out wider.

As the Elders guided us through into the eleventh and twelfth dimensions in 2012, there was simultaneously this expansion of the consciousness levels for many who were pressing up against the Elders below them. For example, a great number of Soul-humans who were in third could align with the momentum of expansion and move into fourth. People in fourth could move into fifth. And so on.

There was this mass movement of energy consciousness expanding beyond what our previous limitations were. Between 2013 and 2015, more Souls started awakening to the eleventh level of consciousness and then to twelfth. And then in this past year of 2016 and into 2017, even more and more Souls are moving into that level of awareness.

CO-CREATING AT ITS BEST

By Dr. Wayne W. Dyer and Esther Hicks

"What happens when you bring together one of the most inspirational spiritual teachers of all time and the Master Sages of the Universe? A magical, insightful, invigorating encounter you will never forget!"

As teachers and guides *"on the leading edge of consciousness,"* Esther Hicks and Dr. Dyer share their wisdom about life here on Earth and beyond as infinite Souls. I was gifted this book from my friend last December, and gobbled it up with the greatest of delight! I have not yet watched the live event from 2013 in California where this conversation actually took place, but reading the written copy of the exchanges in the book, I can feel the joy and deep connection between these two friends.

I have found in my own journey that I often doubt the perfection of it. I question if I am "getting it right" or "making the best choice" in the moment. Witnessing Dr. Dyer's reflections of the winding path he took in this life gave me permission to simply revel in the wonder of my own path. No mistakes. Ever. Just always more Love, more expansion.

Ms. Hicks has also been a guide for me in many moments of confusion, through the wealth of recordings available online from her workshops. Having her guide Dr. Dyer through the wisdom of Abraham only made me love her more – such compassion and insight. This book is pure pleasure!

The eleventh and twelfth dimensions are the Realm of Dreams – the possibility of dreams. It feels like a space where you know dreams come true, where you believe it, where you are playing in the Siddhi realms of mastery in whatever area of play your Soul enjoys.

To quote the title of one of Dr. Wayner Dyer's books – *"I Can See Clearly Now."* In eleven and twelve, yes - you can see clearly now.

You know your place in the Universe as a Soul Guide... a Guide of other Soul-humans.

You are able to track dimensional shifts very clearly, even if you don't quite know what the words for all of it are – you can feel when energies are shifting.

This is such an exciting time for our planet!

The celebration, the joy, the delight in new creations, in new energy... and the celebration by our Elders, by all Souls in how much more creative energy exists in our Universe!

And all from the original Source.

Source sitting at the center of everything... at the center of the Universe... at the center of our Earth... at the center of the work that the Elders are doing.

SOUND HEALING INTEGRATION:

Sarah McLachlan "Answer"

Source vibrates this energy for us of pure appreciation.

Joy, delight!

Source has such delight for the magic of creative energy, for the sparks that are flying when creative energy meets other creative energy and explodes and multiples into new creative energy.

September through December of 2012 was a time of celebration in our Universe by all Souls!

Dancing and celebrating.

And so much joy and love.

An incredible, incredible moment in time!

So the movement was just this pop of the original consciousness edge of ten – this pop into eleven and then stretching out the field into twelve – which gave all of consciousness more room to breathe, to expand, to create new.

Now *(in 2017 when I'm writing this)* a Soul in a human body who is sitting in the consciousness level of eleven or twelve can feel the delight of creative energy. These Souls feel the pure and unified field of Oneness where we are all connected back to the original Source.

There is a gentle flow of aligned energy.

This is a Soul in a human body entering the stream of consciousness where they literally feel like they're floating down the river of knowing, of truth, of love.

There is no end place at which to arrive.

> **There is just Simply**
>
> **The Delight in being Present**
>
> **For this Physical-Spiritual Journey.**

At times, it can feel like you don't belong in this world anymore. People don't get you or you don't get them. There is this big bridge of communication breakdown that feels so real.

But it's simply the speed, the ease with which your system is now operating. It's at a different vibrational level than all of those who aren't yet in the eleventh or twelfth dimension.

The communication gap between someone in the twelfth dimension, for example, and someone in the third or fourth dimension can feel like you're literally Universes away from each other.

SOUND HEALING INTEGRATION:

Ford Atlantic "There is Love"

SO WHAT DO WE DO?

Find examples of Soul-humans you deeply admire and respect for the ways they are walking this Earth… and begin cultivating within yourself those same traits and behaviors.

Speak about Love.

Speak about Truth.

Speak about those matters that are so important to humanity.

Bring through those feelings, sensations, and the wisdom that you know you hold in this higher vibration.

Bring it through your voice, through your words, through your actions, through your creative output.

Bring it through and let it become wisdom that is shared with those around you. Not in a way that you have to save them or fix them or change them or do anything TO anybody else.

ONE DAY

You simply become a channel or conduit of Love flowing through from Source. Through you and out into the world in which we live, with no attachment that it has to do or be anything.

You simply ARE flowing Love.

And then find the ways that feel good to YOU to function in this third dimensional, physical world in which we all chose to live *(yes, you chose it, too, or you wouldn't be here reading this!!)*.

SOUND HEALING INTEGRATION: Ashana "Loving Kindness"

What are those ways that feel good?

Perhaps you need more or better boundaries with the people that you engage with every day. Or perhaps you need more quiet time for contemplation and simply breathing more deeply into your Soul.

I feel like I'm sounding like a broken record by now, but if you haven't fully committed yet to a daily practice of prayer, meditation, exercise, stillness, mindfulness… whatever it is that keeps you embodied and present, this would be the time, *for sure*, to deeply commit to a practice that feels good to you.

My suggestion at this level of consciousness would be *(yes, again!)* Kundalini yoga and Meditation. They are high energy, high vibrational practices that combine the movement of energy and also stillness. Both let you tap into this energy field or stream that you flow in and then find ways to bring that information here into the physical world.

By now, you are hopefully not attached to everyone around you having to understand or agree with what you are seeing so clearly.

You simply become a messenger who has no attachment to where the message goes or who reads it.

You just lovingly deliver the message in whatever way feels best to you.

Now, with technology, we have so many options for how to communicate with people around the world. You don't even need to live near your Tribe in order to have a Tribe. You start holding steady in your own body, feeling your Truth, feeling your alignment with Source, feeling how much access to wisdom about the Universe you have, and trusting how easily and purely it can move through you.

You feel all of that and anchor yourself into a steady vibrational feeling. That vibration goes out and your Tribe will come to you. You will find ways where you will meet with each other, either virtually or physically.

You're not by yourself.

There are energetic signals that we all send out constantly as energetic-spiritual-physical beings. At this level of consciousness, you are connecting in with others who are like you and you will find those Soul-humans with whom you resonate.

You have to be still and quiet and have your daily mindfulness practice in place.

And then trust... trust... know that there is only more.

There is only more from here out.

SOUND HEALING INTEGRATION:

The Head and The Heart
"Let's Be Still"

It is an incredible place to sit and feel and BE love.

To honor the work that your Soul has done that has allowed you to be in this space.

And then honor all that is yet to be created, of which you are a co-creator.

To Be Love.

AFTERGLOW

In life, we are offered moments where we can LEAP! Where we know we are at a crossroads and we can choose the safe, familiar, perhaps easier path. Or straighten our shoulders up, set our eyes far ahead on the horizon, and trust the freefall into the unknown. My suggestion is to always push through our comfort zones and follow what our Soul is whispering we are more than capable of achieving!

I am holding space at the end of this chapter to add stories of Soul-humans who are leaping into the unfamiliar. As consciousness continues to expand, I trust that there will be many, many, many stories to share here. xoxo

Vivienne Gerard

ONE DAY

13-14

THIRTEENTH & FOURTEENTH DIMENSIONS

"The Gift of No Words"

Vivienne Gerard

THIRTEENTH & FOURTEENTH DIMENSIONS

8-8-8… on August 8th of 2015 (an 8 day, 8 month, 8 year), a portal opened energetically for more light to enter our Earth.

Not just a little bit of light – *a flooding of light*.

Eight is a symbol of infinity and on this physical time-date reality with three 8's… consciousness expanded to the thirteenth dimension.

In 2016, consciousness expanded again to the fourteenth dimension. And in November of 2016, yet again to the fifteenth dimension.

I believe that in this year of 2017, we could expand into the sixteenth and then seventeenth dimensions.

This is relevant because of the speed at which it's changing.

We held at the tenth dimension for thousands of years. Then we moved from ten to twelve in just a short amount of time. Then from twelve to fifteen in an even shorter amount of time!

SOUND HEALING INTEGRATION: GuruGanesaha Band "Ma"

So consciousness is expanding more and more rapidly, which is the point of writing this book - to help humans transition through this Soul dimension work.

Because in its human expression, consciousness feels dense and confusing and we don't always remember the Soul level of the shift.

OSHO ZEN TAROT (CARD DECK)

The Transcendental Game of Zen

"When life seems to be full of doubt and uncertainty, we tend to look for a source of inspiration: what will happen in the future? What about my health, the children, what will happen if I make this decision and not that one? This is how the traditional tarot is often used, to satisfy a longing to know about the past and future.

This Osho-Zen Tarot (card deck with illustrations by Ma Deva Padma) focuses instead on gaining an understanding of the **here and now**. *It is a system based on the wisdom of Zen, a wisdom that says events in the outer world simply reflect our own thoughts and feelings, even though we ourselves might be unclear about what those thoughts and feelings are."*

I only own one Tarot Card deck and it is this one that I found in a beautiful store in Encinitas, California two years ago. I recommend it to everyone and many of my friends and clients now have their own set!

It feels important now to hand back any power that you might be offering to me as your Guide in this journey we are taking through *One Day*. YOU are the one in charge of your Soul-human journey. YOU are the one in the driver's seat of your Stories.

So in this final suggested "reading," consider sitting down with this deck of cards and allow YOUR energy to guide you to your own answers. To your own next steps. Deeper and ever deeper into your own wisdom and Knowing.

ONE DAY

Like in all books, we share knowledge and resources through our words. By offering my reflections here, there is information for you to contemplate and then decide if it aligns with your beliefs or not and if there are ways to integrate pieces of what you read.

LANGUAGE OF LOVE

The thirteenth dimension is the playground of Star Beings. On the 8-8-8 portal, there was a call to Star Beings to wake up and start sharing more. In ways that are still unfolding.

As consciousness is evolving, it feels like there aren't words yet for thirteen, fourteen and fifteen.

We communicate in Star Language.

We move to the Universal Language, which is Love.

The language of Stars, a Universal language.

There aren't words for these dimensions.

So then what guidance can we bring to Soul-humans who are still learning or understanding about these advanced dimensions?

SOUND HEALING INTEGRATION:
Bliss
"Grace"

This is the magic of the co-creation.

Once you reach the thirteenth dimension and on, you understand and connect telepathically. You are tapped into the Universal energy field of consciousness... of Stars... of knowledge.

Then it becomes about clarifying YOUR way of interpreting that language. The way that language moves through you in human form. Because that is where you bring your gifts and your wisdom to this Earth to guide those who are still moving through the earlier dimensions.

Thirteen and on is beyond words.

It is beyond illusion.

It is clear knowing without limitation or restriction around it. Words actually take away from the defining and explaining of it.

Allow Sound to Guide You.

SOUND HEALING INTEGRATION:

Caspian
"Hymn for the Greatest Generation"

It's a Feeling. It's warm, like Sunshine.

It's Light... Star... Love... Language.

It's Sacred.

I invite you to pause here to honor the Sacredness of where consciousness began and where it continues to unfold.

SOUND HEALING INTEGRATION:

*Snatam Kaur
"Ong Namo"*

These dimensions are where you practice your own meditation because then you find your own pace and rhythm of alignment with Source energy within.

And you are Guided.

In the thirteenth dimension and on, we offer…

Reverence.

Vivienne Gerard

Reverence for Source.

Reverence for the Original Breath.

Reverence for the Source within each of Us, all of Us.

Reverence for the magnificent Gift of Breath, of Life, of Existence, of Creativity.

Reverence for Light, for Sound.

Reverence for Harmony and Unity.

Reverence for Love.

Vivienne Gerard

What a Gift.

To Be.

To Exist.

AFTERGLOW

Ahhhh... sweet Rachel! There could not be a more perfect example of the complex and delightful joy of consciousness expressed physically in the thirteenth dimension.

I met Rachel two years ago and immediately felt compassion for the human story she shared about losing her husband at a very young age. Now a widow with five children, she was struggling to keep it all together and take care of the needs of each child – along with her own emotional healing. Fiercely independent and very smart, she also intuitively knew things about everyone around her that were spot on... and not always valued when shared.

Rachel is a Star Being, a powerful and wise Guide who is here to help our planet through this shift we are taking. Finally OWNING that for herself is allowing her to now identify what her gifts are and find easier ways to navigate this Soul-human journey.

What freedom! To claim the fullness of who you are and not feel the need to apologize for it or make yourself smaller or less than what you know to be true, just to keep those around you feeling comfortable.

Such a gift to be able to step forward and offer your wisdom! I am bowing to the Beauty that she can share with all of us.

Here is a little of the Clarity that is flowing through and from Rachel, just in the past month:

"I am realizing at a depth how uncomfortable I have physically been since childhood. Sensitive to everything from the seams in my clothing to fluctuating temperatures outside while also seeing and feeling sensations of those around me.

I spent so many years at war with my body, learning to numb it, to disassociate from it.

And while I wouldn't change any of that, the desire to come back to this body, to experience viscerally, physically, all the GOOD things this body can hold, can feel, can experience has completely transformed the structure of my life and my relationships.

That restructuring has been the hardest part.

The part where I have to let go of how I may be perceived, of how I may disappoint, of expanding my capacity to feel good things, to feel loved, to give myself permission to be who I am and feel good while doing it, yet to also feel all the pain and discomfort of getting there, of grieving again and again to make room for new, trusting that the best version of myself must also be what is best for all of those who I love so dearly, whether they see it that way or not.

If there is one thing I want to do with my life, it's that. To show, teach, guide, support, hold space, and love people through the process of learning to love themselves and to love others that deeply.

For me, it keeps coming back to open-hearted individuality that leads to unity. We each have such unique experiences that allow us to bring forward a perspective unlike any other, and solutions unlike any other.

I find that when I try to hold space for all experiences/ perspectives at once, I severely limit my own expression. I become almost muted. My expression becomes watered down, lacking both power and dimension.

It's not a matter of choosing "right" vs. "wrong" or judging any of your behaviors through those lenses, rather choosing the most loving action towards yourself.

The fear that loving yourself could somehow harm another fades away as the separation of "self" and "other" fade away.

What if we could look at all aspects of ourselves as seasonal?

Our interests, our behaviors, our jobs/careers, our location, our relationships, our quirks, our sexuality, our preferences, our identity, our bodies, our perspectives, our beliefs.

ONE DAY

What if it was all seasonal, passing by to come again a bit differently? What if the only thing that was true or real, the only thing to cling onto was now?

This moment.

This expression.

This feeling.

This me.

This other.

This thought.

This idea.

This room.

This bowl of soup.

Never to be experienced quite the same again.

A Gift in Time.

No matter the words, the language, the lens, it all comes back to the same thing.

Call it science. Call it religion. Call it conspiracy. Call it perfection. Call it evolution. Call it healing. Call it psychology. Call it astrology. It doesn't matter.

We are Moving.

And while it may seem like we're all Moving in different directions, we are all going to the same place.

And where we are going, it is GOOD."

Vivienne Gerard

15...

FIFTEENTH DIMENSION AND BEYOND

"Love"

Vivienne Gerard

FIFTEENTH DIMENSION AND BEYOND

SOUND HEALING INTEGRATION:
Chrvches "Afterglow"

AFTERGLOW

And so I sit here at the edge of consciousness, holding space with the Elders, for and with our Gaia Tribe.

Knowing that all is well and exactly as it is meant to be – the most perfect of ever-flowing co-creations unfolding, moment by moment in this beautiful Now.

My heart is full... steady... eager for all that is yet to come.

I chose this experience of incarnation with the greatest of care, trusting that all Souls on Earth also arrived with me in the seeking of our highest potential, and knowing that I would create this very moment of birthing new into existence.

In this moment, I sit here in front of my computer knowing that this book's Journey of Creation is almost complete as I transcribe Source energy into words.

Precise in each choice.

Exhaling with delight in the joy of this spiritual-physical dance.

What a gift to flow this Pure Love through to you.

...

And now we play!

And co-create More

Upon More

Upon More

...

EPILOGUE

SOUND HEALING INTEGRATION:

Coldplay
~'Til Kingdom Come~

And so we end as we began...
with sound. xoxo

Vivienne Gerard

RESOURCES

Vivienne Gerard

RESOURCES

SUGGESTED READINGS

Dyer, Dr. Wayne W. and Esther Hicks. *Co-creating at Its Best: A Conversation Between Master Teachers.* Carlsbad, California: Hay House, Inc, 2014.

Emoto, Masaru. *The True Power of Water: Healing and Discovering Ourselves.* Hillsboro, Oregon: Beyond Words Publishing, Inc., 2005.

Hay, Louise L. *You Can Heal Your Life.* Carlsbad, California: Hay House, Inc, 2004.

Hendricks, Gay. *The Big Leap: Conquer Your Hidden Fear and Take Life to the Next Level.* New York, New York: HarperCollins Publishers, 2009.

Higashida, Naoki and KA. *The Reason I Jump: The Inner Voice of a Thirteen-Year-Old Boy with Autism.* New York, New York: Random House, 2016.

Lesser, Elizabeth. *Broken Open: How Difficult Times Can Help Us Grow.* New York, New York: Villard, 2008.

Newton, Michael. *Journey of Souls: Case Studies of Life Between Lives.* Woodbury, Minnesota: Llewellyn Publications, 2013.

Osho and Ma Deva Padma. *Osho Zen Tarot: The Transcendental Game Of Zen.* New York, New York: St Martin's Press, 1994.

Pond, David. *Chakras For Beginners: A Guide to Balancing Your Chakra Energies.* Woodbury, Minnesota: Llewellyn Publications, 2011.

Rudd, Richard. *The Gene Keys: Unlocking the Higher Purpose Hidden in Your DNA*. London, UK: Watkins Publishing, 2015.

Schwartz, Robert. *Your Soul's Plan: Discovering the Real Meaning of the Life You Planned Before You Were Born*. Berkeley, California: Frog Books, 2009.

Singer, Michael A. *The Surrender Experiment: My Journey into Life's Perfection*. New York, New York: Harmony Books, 2015.

SUGGESTED SOUNDS

The Ho'oponopono Song

Alicia Mathewson: *Breathe In Breathe Out, Sweet September*

Anugama: *Chakra Journey*

Ashana: *Into Your Arms, Kyrie, Loving Kindness*

Avicii: *Wake Me Up*

Bachan Kaur: *Forgiveness*

Bliss: *Grace, I'll be waiting*

Caspian: *Hymn for the Greatest Generation, Rioseco, Separation, Waking Season*

Christina Aguilera: *Cruz, I'm Ok, The Voice Within*

Chrvches: *Afterglow, Clearest Blue*

Coldplay: *Speed of Sound, 'Til Kingdom Come, Yellow*

Craig Pruess, Ananda: *Devi Prayer*

Crown of Eternity: *Ang Sang Wahe Guru, Ra Ma Da Sa*

David Ramirez: *Fire of Time*

ONE DAY

Deuter: *Gaia dreaming herself awake, Temple of Silence*

Donna DeLory: *Blessed Always, In the Sun*

Fleetwood Mac: *Songbird*

Ford Atlantic: *Let your heart hold fast, There is Love*

GuruGanesha Singh: *In the light of My Soul, Ma*

Imagine Dragons: *Bleeding Out, Friction, It's Time, Trouble*

John Lennon: *Imagine*

Katy Perry: *Roar*

Keane: *Somewhere only we know*

Liquid Bloom: *Roots of the Earth, Whispers of our Ancestors*

My Soul Journey (Viv Gerard): *Changing the Story, Energy Flowing, Feeling the Love, Muscle Testing, Nothing Becomes Everything, Purifying Breath, Soul Filters' Story*

National Geographic Channel: *Before the Flood*

Nirinjan Kaur: *Kirtan Kriya*

Rafael Bejarano: *Ofrende a la Madre Tierra*

Sarah McLachlan: *Answer*

Snatam Kaur: *Again and Again, Carry Me, Heart of the Universe, Long Time Sun, Ong Namo*

Temper Trap: *Alive, So Much Sky*

The Head and the Heart: *Let's be Still*

The Lumineers: *Stubborn Love*

The Moody Blues: *Question*

U2: *Song for Someone*

Vivienne Gerard

ONE DAY

THE SOUL FILTERS' STORY

Vivienne Gerard

THE SOUL FILTERS' STORY

(Transcribed from the original recording)

Once upon a time... a long, long time ago, the Original Breath of Life started in a Star.

And that Star got bigger and bigger and bigger and filled with more and more Helium and Hydrogen until it exploded!

And when it exploded, it created more Stars!

> SOUND HEALING INTEGRATION:
> MSJ YouTube "Soul Filters' Story"

And the Stars were dancing and playing in the Universe and there were more Stars and more Stars. The Stars started to gather and they would form these Constellations, like Orion. And the Stars would create these new ways of being together.

Eventually, more and more Stars exploded and got created and exploded and got created and they started to bump together and form these dense conglomerates of energy that they called Planets.

Then the Planets started moving in rotation around the grandest of the Stars, the Sun. They were just orbiting around and as they did that, these other particles stared to gather and they clumped together. They called themselves Moons and they started to rotate around the planets, within the orbit, going around the Sun.

Then the story continued with the Ring. The Planets that were on the outermost edge of all this orbiting were large and filled with lots of gas. The astroids and comets and energies that were floating around – the stardust out in the galaxy – started to bump against those outermost Planets. The Planets didn't like that and so they started to press out those pieces and they formed these swirling, twirling energies that they called Rings.

And so the Universe was created.

In all of this, consciousness started to spread. Consciousness was individual, individual, individual, individual... but there was this collective energy of all of consciousness working together to continue expanding the Universe.

Pretty soon, consciousness in the individual form was saying *"We should go play on some of these planets and see if we can practice expanding the Universe in a more physical form.*

So we're going to need a way to dull our brilliance so as we arrive on the planet, we have some way of engaging with the physical. Because our brilliant conscious selves know everything, so we have to have a way to mask or hide it in the physical form to explore what it is like to be consciousness in the physical.

What we're going to do is use these cosmic beings that we're already familiar with and comfortable with as patterns for how we're going to filter our soul when we arrive on the planet of Earth."

...

The **Star Filter** raised his hand and said: *"I'll go first, I'll go first!"* The Star Filter put on this shroud and arrived on the Earth and said *"WOAHHH... this is way different than what I thought it was going to be when I was a Star out in the Universe. It's a little dense, it's a little scary, it's a lot aggressive, people do not understand me. They don't see my brilliance. I'd better hide it because I don't want to get discovered for being so brilliant."* So the Star Filter started to walk on Earth, hiding his brilliance.

The next one that raised her hand was the **Orion Filter**. She said, *"Wait, wait, I know how to create constellations."* So a

ONE DAY

Soul that puts on the Orion Filter comes to Earth and knows that there's this possibility of creating something new that has never existed before by seeing the brilliance within individual Stars and gathering them together. Forming communities and pathways and ways of communicating and creating that have never existed before.

But when they're here, they're like *"Where is everybody? Why isn't anybody here? I thought we were going to have these constellations. Nobody's paying attention to me! Wait, wait!"* And they start to force their will on other people to try to create something instead of just holding steady and magnetizing the other Stars towards them. And so the Orion Filters start to walk around the Earth all confused.

Then the **Planet Filter** raises its hand and says *"I'll go next!"* The Souls put on the Planet Filter and they know when they arrive on Earth, the Planets are grounded and solid and they have their known ways of doing things and they go around Earth in this direction and they know what to do and how it's going to go. And so the Planet Filter arrives on Earth and says *"I know the way! Follow me, everybody, this is the way we do it!"* And then people tell them they're wrong and they don't understand and no, they don't know what they do.

So the Planet Filter starts to feel betrayed and they're like *"Wait a second, no-one's listening to me. I'm going to have to control what they say and do so they'll listen to me."* And so they start to force other people. And chaos ensues! And the Planet Filters are walking around Earth.

The **Moon Filter** says *"I can go fix it all! I know exactly what to do!"* And the Moon Filter arrives on Earth saying *"Everybody, everybody… I can see the light and the shadow, I'm the Moon! I hold all lights and when I'm moving around the orbit of the Planet, when I'm doing my job in relationship with other people, I know when it's Light and I know when it's Shadow, so follow me!"*

And then people start to follow and the Moon is like *"Oh wait, where's light and where's shadow and why isn't the Planet doing what it said it would do. I don't understand why everything is so chaotic! Aghh!"* And they start to shrink and hide because they're so scared they'll get it wrong. And so the Moon Filters start to walk around the Earth so confused because it wasn't what it was supposed to be!

So the **Ring Filter** raises its hand – *"I know how to have fun and how to make it all better. I'm the Ring, I'm flashy and exciting and adventurous! Follow me, people! I'm the last one, remember? I take all the stardust and I collect it from where it's been spinning around the world and I know how to fix it! I am the hero and I can save the day! Watch! I'll go!"* And so the Hero, the Ring Filter arrives on Earth and says *"Hey everybody, let's have some fun! Let's play! Come on, people! I know how to make everyone feel better. We'll make it an adventure! Follow me, follow me!"*

And so they try to show how easy and amazing the journey is supposed to be. But everyone else is already in their wound and shadow and *saying "It's not easy, it's not fun. This is not the way it's supposed to be."* And so the Ring Filter says *"Oh, I did it wrong. No, that doesn't feel right. I don't think anyone actually believes in me. I don't know if I believe in me. I'd better do what I'm supposed to do. I'll just follow along with everybody else and go into the Shadow."*

And all of these beautiful Souls are here on Earth with all of these Filters, stumbling around in the shadow, knowing they have this brilliant, incredible gift inside of them. But they don't know how to share it or uncover it.

And so the adventure and the journey begins.

That is what the human experience is about: uncovering the Shadow to find the Light, to find the Gift of the Soul Filter. Because when you do that, when you go in and you see and you remember who you really are, who you agreed to be before you put on the Filter and arrived here on

Earth, what we start to uncover is that we're ALL connected. We're ALL part of this collective.

> We're ALL just Love and Consciousness Seeking to Expand And to Bring All of Our Individual Gifts to this Collective Moment of NOW.

So, the work… the work of the human that is a Soul with a Filter on it, is to go IN DEEP and uncover what the gift is that they came here to bring.

When we step into the space of harmony, when each soul understands it's Filter and takes the Filter Shadow off and shines the brilliance of the Filter Gift…

We start to have the greatest harmony that could possibly exist on planet Earth:

A *Star Filter* in its brilliance, lighting the way, showing humans what is possible, what can be seen as shared through Source's eyes. What Source is sending down into this Earth. The Star can see it, translate it, and share it with Humanity.

When it's shared, the *Orion Filter* can listen to all of these brilliant, powerful, knowledgeable Stars and go *"Wait – I see the pattern! I understand! And if everybody can listen, I can tell you what the greatest possibility is that we could weave. You and you and you and you – bring your brilliance together and look at what you can create that's never existed before!"* All of these Stars start to gather and they're creating all of these patterns, guided by the Orion Filter. And it's good!

And then the *Planet Filter* goes *"I know how to help! I can GROUND the energy. I can ground the energy of this new constellation here on Earth. I can show you to anchor it into this moment, this body. And because I'm a fighter and a courageous one who perseveres in all of my endeavors, watch — I will show you how to fight and how to push, how to collaborate with strength so that we actually achieve that thing that we see can be created."*

And so as the Planet grounds, the *Moon Filter* brings in its gift and says *"I see the Light and the Shadow. I see the balance between the Masculine and the Feminine. I see the possibilities and the realities, all blended together. Let me help guide you in how to find balance in this beautiful idea that the Stars and the Orions have brought forward and the Planets have grounded."*

As the Moon brings her Light and awareness and her gifts of balance and space-holding into this collaboration of the greatest harmony possible on the planet, the *Ring Filter* comes in with all of its adventure and play and joy and says *"Yes, this is what I came here for! I remember. I remember I came here to show you that the Ring in its solidness is a symbol of infinity and we last forever when we all work together in this greatest harmony of the Universe, here represented on planet Earth."*

And so it is. And so it expands.

And more and more and more Consciousness and Love is created as each Soul steps from their Shadow into their Gift and works together for the greatest Harmony.

To learn more about the Soul Filters and explore the resources that are available to support you in *Your* Soul Journey, please visit:

www.mysouljourney.com

ABOUT THE AUTHOR

Vivienne Gerard is a Healer, Guide, and Lover of Souls and Humanity. An Orion-Moon Soul Filter, she is gifted at recognizing the brilliance in those around her and then finding the ways to connect them together to form new constellations here on Earth.

Viv leads **Viben**, a weekly group meditation call on Sundays that taps into what is shifting on our planet in the NOW moment. She also hosts monthly **Viben Circles** on the New Moon, guiding participants to clarify and claim their intentions for the month ahead. And Viv offers private coaching for Soul-humans who are ready to *"clear past patterns and co-create a more empowered Now."*

Simply for pleasure, Viv interviews ordinary yet extraordinary people about their stories in an ongoing video series titled **Healing Our Souls**. You can also follow her weekly blog of **Reflections** on her website.

Viv's greatest Loves are her husband, Brad, and her two children, Callie and Ryan. They live in Cincinnati, Ohio, with their cat, Katniss, and their dog, Star.

Life is Good!

Vivienne Gerard

This IS
Our
Happily
Ever After!

Made in the USA
Lexington, KY
13 April 2017